Trans-Africa Motoring

Dedicated
in loving memory
to Alec, Sis and to my father
who all contributed in their own way

By the same author:
Trans-Asia Motoring

Trans-Africa Motoring

Colin McElduff

WILTON HOUSE GENTRY · LONDON

Published by Wilton House Gentry Limited,
85 Gloucester Road, London SW7.
Designed by Brian Roll.
Filmset by V. Siviter Smith & Co. Ltd.,
Birmingham, England.
Printed and bound in Great Britain by
William Clowes & Sons, Limited,
London, Beccles and Colchester.

Contents

Part 5/General Information on Countries

Part 6/Currency Regulations

Part 7/Regulations and Information for Crossing the Sahara

Part 8/North Africa: West-East Routes and Information

Illustrations

Maps

Cartographers: C. Martin Daine and Colin McElduff

Acknowledgments

My aim in compiling this book has been to provide travellers visiting the African continent – and overlanders in general – with the information and details they need to achieve a successful and enjoyable journey through difficult terrain. As I am no stranger to Africa, my task has been greatly reduced, for many of my old compatriots came forth with invaluable help. I wish therefore to thank Tim and Peter Bailey, John Price and Keith Meadows who lent me photographs and who travelled over many of the routes and supplied reports on them. A special mention of thanks is due to the impeccable William H. Lee whose doggedness in obtaining information became legend.

I am grateful to the National Tourist Offices, High Commissions and Embassies for information concerning their countries, and to the Department of Trade in the United Kingdom who provided details on currencies. I wish also to thank the Royal Automobile Club who supplied the main impetus in the writing of this book.

I am indebted to the United Nations Economic Commission for Africa in Addis Ababa who so kindly read my precis and whose observations helped me and urged me on to complete the task.

There are also many others, travellers and adventurers, without whose help and encouragement this book would never have been written.

Colin McElduff F.R.G.S.

Introduction

This book has been compiled to fulfil the trans-African motorist's need for accurate information and advice, to enable him to plan, prepare and achieve a better understanding of the undertaking ahead of him.

The continent of Africa as a whole still presents a challenge, and for most people remains one of the last great motoring adventures. Within Africa, there are regions of antiquity, shrouded in mystery, huge wildernesses and jungle fastnesses untouched by modern times, in which the combined land masses of Europe, the United States, India, New Zealand and Japan would be completely lost. In short, Africa is big. There are still areas where the European is a rarity, and where his arrival is greeted by the inhabitants with great interest and courtesy.

Because of the many hazards that may be met on an overland journey, it is extremely important that the venture is planned on an expedition basis. It must not be undertaken lightly.

Some routes in desolate regions are not recommended, especially for the inexperienced traveller. Routes in these hazardous areas should always be checked first with local authorities and their advice taken, as changes occur quickly. It is essential that the vehicle to be used should have a high ground clearance, be sturdy, and have a good spares potential. It should also be equipped with adequate fuel, water, spares and emergency equipment. Reports are often

The continent of Africa presents one of the last great motoring chal-lenges. The treacherous dunes of the Grand Erg Occidental in Algeria, viewed from the track between Guerzim and El Quata (above) form a stark contrast to the luxuriant rain forests of Zaire, (below), viewed from a first-class earth road between Buta and Bambessa.

received of vehicles being abandoned and of the unwary traveller dying of thirst or heat exhaustion in Saharan regions. In most cases, such events are brought about purely by bad planning and a lack of appreciation of the difficulties to be encountered.

It is therefore vital that the trans-African traveller learns as much as possible about the geography of the countries he intends to visit, and of the people in them, together with the climatic conditions and the prevailing political situation.

Whilst every effort has been made to provide accurate and up-to-date information in this book, no claims whatsoever can be made for any delay, inconvenience, loss or damage from its use.

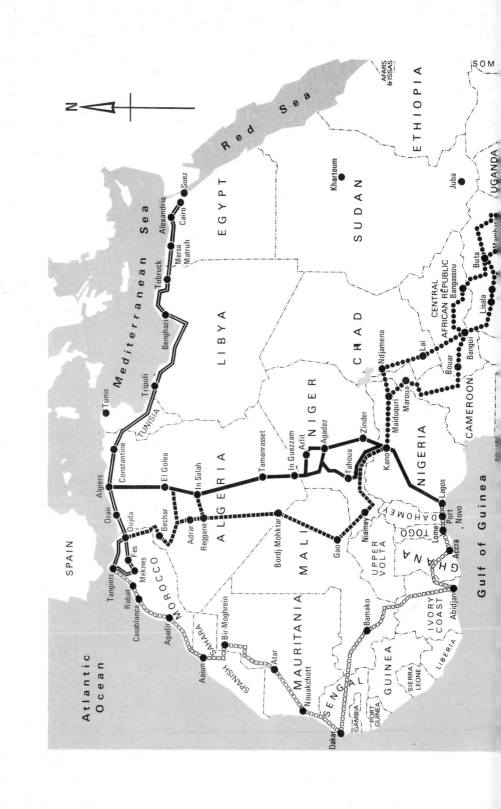

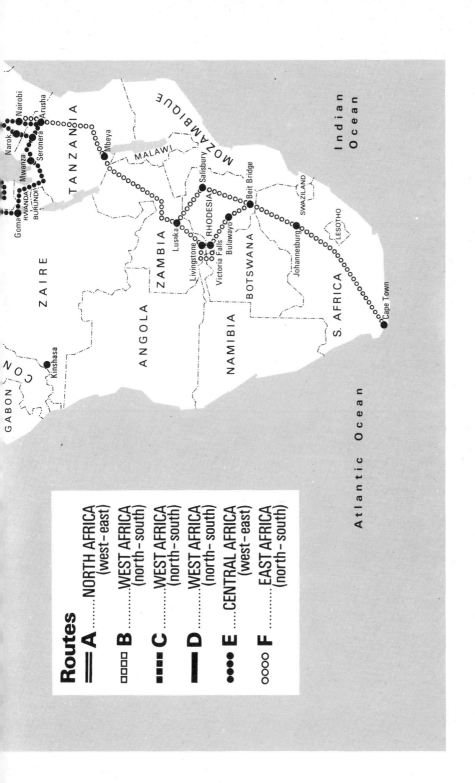

Routes

A .... NORTH AFRICA (west–east)

B .... WEST AFRICA (north–south)

C .... WEST AFRICA (north–south)

D .... WEST AFRICA (north–south)

E .... CENTRAL AFRICA (west–east)

F .... EAST AFRICA (north–south)

Part 1
Planning

Basic Route

An overland journey to South Africa offers limitless possibilities, and the exact route you decide to take will obviously be dictated by personal preference, financial resources, and the length of time available to you. The most popular route is to start in North Africa, take one of the Saharan routes to Nigeria, go east to Kenya and thence southwards. However, travellers with more time–and money–at their disposal may choose an exciting alternative, via Eastern Europe to the Middle East and on to India, thence by sea to East Africa and southwards.

The basic trans-African route falls naturally into three phases. Phase one begins in Tangiers, Algeria and ends in Kano, Nigeria. This is the trans-Saharan phase and is extremely hazardous in the Saharan deep south. Distances between inhabited areas increase as one travels south, from 300, 400, to 540 miles. Inhabited areas mean 'back up', which means fuel, water, spares and food. The range of the vehicle must therefore be increased to at least 700 miles, as adequate reserves of fuel must be carried for back-tracking purposes in case one loses the desert-track beacons or gets into soft ground.

Phase two begins in Kano, Nigeria and ends in Nairobi, Kenya. This is the central African phase which can present many hazardous obstacles, such as river crossings, precarious bridges and appalling road conditions. Shortages of fuel supplies will also be experienced, especially in Zaire (Congo), as many of the smaller petrol stations in villages are no longer supplied.

Phase three begins in Nairobi, Kenya and ends in the Republic of South Africa. This is the East to South Africa phase, and is the least difficult of the three roadwise, as almost the whole of the journey can be accomplished on good sealed roads with adequate 'back up'. The only difficulties the traveller may experience are political, and you should ensure you have accurate information on the conditions prevailing at the time you travel.

A more detailed itinerary for this route is as follows:

Tangiers–along coast to Algiers–across the Sahara on the Hoggar route, via El Golea, In Salah, Tamanrasset, Agadez to Kano–eastwards to East Africa, via Ndjamena (Fort Lamy), Bangui, Buta, Mambasa, Beni, Goma, Ruhengeri, Kigali,

Rusumo, Mwansa, Seronera, Arusha, to Nairobi–southwards to Cape Town.

Basic distance:	approx. 10,000 miles
Plus 10% margin:	1,000 miles
U.K. to Tangiers:	approx. 1,200 miles
Total:	12,200 miles

Details of all the main routes across the African continent, including mileages between all main towns, are given in Parts 8—11 of this book (pages 137–207), and you should study these pages carefully before deciding on your own particular itinerary. Additional information on crossing the Sahara is given in Part 7 (pages 127–135). In particular, you should pay special attention to the type of road over which your selected route takes you–the key on the left-hand side of each of the route pages gives an immediate indication of this. Remember that driving on desert or dirt tracks can prove an exhausting and hazardous experience for even the most experienced overlander. For a successful and enjoyable journey, you must take a realistic approach to your vehicle's–and your own–limitations.

Diagrammatic maps appear at the beginning of each of the route sections, showing each of the routes described. Initially, you may find it more useful to consult the map of Africa as a whole, on pages 14–15.

Political Restrictions

At present, an overland journey to East and South Africa is only possible via one of the trans-Saharan routes and on the major road networks through the countries of Algeria, Niger, Nigeria, Cameroun, Tchad, Central African Republic, Zaire, Rwanda, Tanzania and Kenya. Political instability, confrontation, drought or famine prevent or make it very unwise to travel through Angola, Egypt, Ethiopia, Mozambique, Sudan or Uganda. The restricted use of the Suez Canal and the Arab–Israeli confrontation has made it very difficult to by-pass Egypt and the Sudan by way of the Red Sea and Saudi Arabia. This latter country discourages motorists in transit and has no touristic facilities other than those for the

Moslem pilgrims visiting the holy places in Mecca and Medina.

In a book of this nature, it is impossible to give absolutely up-to-the-minute information on the political status of individual countries. Governments can be deposed practically over-night; border confrontations can develop in an equally short space of time. Thus, as a matter of common sense, you should keep yourself informed of the latest political situation in each of the countries you intend to visit. If you are in any doubt as to the wisdom of travelling through any particular country, the obvious answer is–don't! If you should become caught up in any politically explosive situation, you should contact your nearest embassy or consul at once (see pages 214–224 for addresses and telephone numbers), but remember that they may not always be able to give you immediate practical assistance.

When to go

A journey from Europe to East and South Africa is best undertaken between October and April. You should at all costs avoid the rainy season: in West Africa, this lasts from May to the end of September;

The appalling road conditions that may be encountered after the rainy season, between Alimbongo and Lubero, Zaire.

RAIN CHART

	JANUARY	FEBRUARY	MARCH	APRIL	MAY	JUNE	JULY	AUGUST	SEPTEMBER	OCTOBER	NOVEMBER	DECEMBER
NORTH AFRICAN DESERT.....	PRACTICALLY NO RAIN					SAHARA CLOSED BY HEAT						
WEST AFRICA						▨	▨	▨	▨	▨		
EQUATORIAL AFRICA........			▨	▨			█	█	▨	▨	▨	
SOUTHERN SUDAN..........					▨	▨	▨	▨	▨			
NORTHERN NIGERIA........				▨	▨	▨	▨	▨	▨			
NORTHERN ZAIRE	▨	▨	RAIN AT INTERVALS THROUGHOUT YEAR						▨	▨	▨	▨
SOUTHERN ZAIRE	█	▨	▨							▨	▨	▨
UGANDA			▨	█	█	▨	▨		▨	▨	▨	
KENYA			▨	█	█					▨	▨	▨
NORTHERN TANZANIA			▨	█	▨						▨	▨
CENTRAL TANZANIA........	█	▨	▨	▨	▨							▨
SOUTHERN TANZANIA	▨	▨	█	▨	▨							▨
ZAMBIA....................	█	█	▨								▨	▨
MALAWI	█	█	▨									▨
RHODESIA..................	█	█	▨								▨	▨
TRANSVAAL, NATAL, O.F.S.	▨	▨	▨								▨	▨
CAPE PROVINCE (EASTERN)	▨								▨	▨	▨	▨
CAPE PROVINCE (WESTERN)				▨	▨	▨	▨	▨				

KEY

☐ DRY MONTHS

▨ RAINY SEASON LIGHT TO MODERATE RAINS

█ RAINY SEASON HEAVY RAINS

IT MUST HOWEVER BE REMEMBERED THAT THE AFRICAN CLIMATE IS IN GENERAL UNCERTAIN AND WET WEATHER MAY BE EXPERIENCED DURING THE PERIODS SHOWN AS DRY AND VICE VERSA.

in Central Africa, it rains throughout the year, but extremely heavy rainfall occurs between September and October and between May and June.

The Sahara is at its coolest between December and January, and at this time of year the likelihood of sandstorms is also eliminated. The worst time of year to cross the Sahara, in view of the intense heat and frequent sandstorms, is during the period 1st June–15th September; permission to travel can in fact be refused at this time.

Visits to North Africa are best made in the early spring or autumn, thus avoiding the extreme heat of midsummer.

For more detailed information on the climates of individual countries, you should refer to Part 5 (pages 79–108).

Time to Allow

It is not possible to provide detailed information on how long it will take to motor across Africa because of the varying types of conditions that will be encountered. As a general rule, you should allow 8 weeks for a journey from the United Kingdom to Nairobi, East Africa, and 12 weeks to Cape Town, South Africa. This assumes approximately 36 hours' driving a week–i.e. six hours daily for six days, followed by one day's rest.

In order to work out a more detailed schedule, tailored to the particular route you choose, you should consult the route sections on pages 137–207. These show mileages between towns and the type of road on which you will be driving. Driving times are given where practical, but in many cases this will depend very much upon the type of vehicle and, on rough roads and tracks, upon the surface conditions and weather which may, of course, vary considerably from week to week.

As a rough guide, you may expect to average 30 to 40 mph on sealed roads–i.e. tarmac or asphalt surfaces–although in really good conditions you may achieve much more; on gravel surfaces, from 20 to 30 mph; and on desert and dirt tracks only 10 to 20 mph. In the Saharan deep south, 140 miles may take from 6 to 7 hours' driving. Thus, a journey from the United Kingdom to Lagos, Nigeria may take 21 days, whilst Algeria to Kano may take 8 to 12 days. By studying carefully the information given in the route sections, however, you should be able to work out a practical schedule to cover the entire journey.

Finance

It is not possible to provide true and accurate costs for an overland journey across Africa because of the ever-changing conditions that will be encountered. Local price variations, weather conditions, road conditions, political developments–all these factors can affect the ultimate cost of the journey as a whole, and all are of course impossible to anticipate to any degree of accuracy. Again, the overwhelming variety in possible itineraries makes any journey across Africa very much a matter of personal choice–no two routes are likely to be exactly the same.

The basic operational costs of a 12-week trans-African journey for a party of four, following the basic itinerary described on page 19, are given at the end of this section. It should be emphasized, however, that these figures are to be taken *as a guide only*. Specifically, you are advised to make your own calculations for total fuel consumption and personal expenses if the details of the itinerary you have selected differ significantly from those cited. Hints on how to make these calculations are given below.

You should constantly bear in mind the fact that an overland journey across Africa is *not* the cheapest method of travelling! Although it is only too tempting to cut down on funds–especially those allotted as 'spending' money and other incidental expenses– you must be realistic. Remember, too, that unforeseeable emergencies can happen–and will often demand an immediately accessible reserve of funds. Nothing is more likely to wreck your enjoyment of the journey as a whole than a shortage of cash.

As fuel will take up a significant proportion of the total cost of your journey, it is worth making some fairly detailed calculations on your total estimated consumption. First, decide on the route you will be taking and, by referring to the route sections on pages 137–207, add up your mileage. For ease of reference, a precis of the total mileages between main towns is listed at the beginning of each of the four sections. Remember to include the mileage between your point of departure and your first port of call in Africa. Add on a 10 per cent safety margin.

The rate of fuel consumption will obviously depend upon the type of vehicle you intend to drive. The chart below gives figures for all the most suitable types of vehicle. In each case, you are advised to take the figure for minimum fuel consumption: this applies to motoring under adverse conditions (i.e. four-wheel drive in the Sahara) and although such conditions obviously will not apply throughout your journey, this figure builds in a sensible fail-safe for costing purposes.

Vehicle	Specification	Fuel	Overall mpg	Cruising/ typical mpg	Minimum mpg
Land Rover					
88SWB:	4-cyl 2286 cc	Petrol	18	17·4	12
109LWB:	6-cyl 2625 cc	Petrol	14·9	15·9	10
109LWB:	4-cyl 2286 cc	Diesel	25·5	21	16
B.L.M.C.					
J4-JU250:	4-cyl 1622 cc	Petrol	18	20	12
Chevrolet					
G30 Van:	V8 engine	Petrol	15·8	17·8	10
Commer:	4-cyl 1725 cc	Petrol	20·2	19	14
Fiat:	4-cyl 850-903 cc	Petrol	34·1	35	25
Ford Escort:	4-cyl 1098 cc	Petrol	31·5	35·6	20
	4-cyl 1300 cc	Petrol	26·7	28	17
	4-cyl 1600 cc	Petrol	21·5	22	14
Transit:	4-cyl 1663-1993-2495 cc	Petrol		22	14
Mercedes					
Benz:	4-cyl 2-197 cc	Petrol	20·2	22	14
Toyota					
1600ST:	4-cyl 1588 cc	Petrol	28	30	18
V.W. Camper:	4-cyl 1795 cc	Petrol	21·3	23	14

You should now be able to work out your total fuel requirements. The cost per gallon of fuel is subject to considerable fluctuations across the African continent, and again you must build a fail-safe into your calculations. It would not be realistic to assume less than

75p per gallon for petrol, and a third less (i.e. 50p) per gallon for diesel.

Thus, to recap, you should assess fuel consumption on the minimum your vehicle will return under adverse conditions, and multiply this by the fail-safe price per gallon given above. This may seem an over-cautious method of calculation, but remember that lengthy detours may be forced upon you, however well you plan your route, and that even the most experienced map reader is liable to come seriously adrift in the Sahara. By using this method you should find, however, that you have adequate reserves of cash available for other funds, should it be needed, once your journey is half-completed.

Personal expenses will obviously depend to a great extent upon the duration of your journey. The 12-week period cited in the basic costs given below is based on a total mileage of 13,000 miles, following the basic itinerary given on page 19 and allowing approximately 36 hours' driving per week. It is not advisable to attempt to pack in more driving than this (see 'Daily Routine' page 61), but should you decide to take things at a slower pace, you will of course have to recalculate the total duration of the journey. If your proposed route is substantially different to the one cited below, you should consult the section 'Time to Allow' on page 23.

It is reasonable to assume a cost of £1.00 per person per day to cover food, medicine, etc.–i.e. the cost of keeping the passengers going. This does assume a fairly simple life style–preparing your own food in camp and not eating out at expensive restaurants.

Additional expenses will include the cost of the vehicle, Carnets de Passages, vehicle and personal/medical insurance, game-park fees, ferries across rivers, toll bridges, camping, gratuities, pocket money. . .

The figures below give the basic operational costs, for four persons, of a 12-week trans-African journey following the basic itinerary described on page 19, and allowing approximately 36 hours' driving per week. The capital costs of acquiring and equipping a vehicle are not included.

Petrol: 13,000 miles at 10 miles to the gallon, assuming petrol at 75p per gallon: £975
Lubricants, etc. for vehicle (note: oil may be obtained duty-free in Ceuta): £30

Sea transportation for vehicle and passengers, across the Channel and Mediterranean: £59

Spare parts, including tyres (new tyres are essential): £240

Sundry vehicle maintenance, breakdowns, etc. (this figure is optimistic: it may well come to more): £100

Cost of visas (certain nationals may have to pay more): £20

Cost of keeping passengers going (food, medicine, etc.) at £1.00 per person per day: £336

Sufficient funds to comply with any governmental regulations en route and for entry into South Africa, at £200 reserve per person: £800

Total cost: £2,560

per person: £640

You should take adequate amounts of currency, as well as traveller's cheques, for the journey. Sterling bank notes, dollar bills and West German marks are generally accepted in those areas where there are no facilities for cashing traveller's cheques. Whilst it is prudent to carry the currency of the country you are passing through, it should be remembered that most countries do not allow the export of their own currency. (Information on currency regulations by country are given in Part 6, pages 109–125). So when obtaining traveller's cheques from your bank, remember to get some small denominations. Traveller's cheques should be obtained from banks that are known world-wide. American Express, Cooks, Barclays and Lloyds are commonly recognised by all foreign banks.

Embassies, Consulates and High Commissions abroad will always assist their nationals in an emergency. (A list of addresses for British, Irish, Australian, Canadian and American representatives in Africa is given on pages 214–224.) However, they are *not* travel bureaux, and should not be expected to lend money to disorganised travellers who are unable to afford the return fare home. Thus, you must ensure that your financial reserve is sufficient to cater for all emergencies.

Shipping Onwards

If you intend to ship onwards from Africa, either to continue your journey in Australia or India, or to return home, you should make the necessary arrangements before you begin your journey. Shipping space for vehicles and passengers is not easy to acquire, and it is always advisable to make the bookings well in advance.

Shipping Agents in U.K.:

Lloyd Triestino,
Thomas Cook (agents),
45 Berkeley Street,
London W1A 1EB.
Tel: 01-499 4000
(depart from Italy)

Southern Ferries,
Arundel Towers,
Portland Terrace,
Southampton.
Tel: Southampton (0703) 34141
(to Tangiers only)

Union Castle Line,
Chief Passenger Office,
Rotherwick House,
19-21 Old Bond Street,
London W1X 4AN.
Tel: 01-493 8400

Shipping Agents in South Africa:

Lloyd Triestino,
Castlemarine (Pty) Ltd,
53 St George's Street,
P.O. Box 7,
Cape Town,
South Africa.
Tel: 41 3451

P & O Passenger Division,
Musgrove & Watson (Pty) Ltd.,
Pearl Assurance House,
Heerengracht Foreshore,
P.O. Box 702,
Cape Town,
South Africa.
Tel: 45 3331

Union Castle Line,
Castlemarine,
53 St George's Street,
Cape Town,
South Africa.
Tel: 41 3451

Note: a recent reduction in the number of vessels sailing to Australasia via South Africa has made bookings very difficult to obtain in South Africa.

Travelling Companions

Remember that the characters of the people travelling in your party form a vitally important ingredient, which can make or mar the entire journey. Any haphazard mix of personalities will soon be exposed in the cramped confines of a Land Rover or similar vehicle–your virtual home for much of the entire journey–and can all too easily spell disaster.

Children below the age of seven should not be taken on extended overland journeys across Africa. It is difficult to protect very young children against heat, infection and disease, and to ensure that they maintain an adequate fluid intake. Babies will suffer cruelly from prickly heat.

Age in itself is not a deciding factor for the journey; however, all travellers must be fit and able to stand the rigours of digging, pushing and lifting when a vehicle gets stuck in difficult ground.

Persons suffering from an acute ailment should not travel, as treatment may be completely unavailable in some regions.

Reading List

You should learn as much as you can about the different countries you will be visiting. Any information you can acquire relating to local customs will prove especially rewarding, as these vary immensely throughout the African continent. The publications listed below are all recommended, and should be available through your public library.

Africa (magazine) (African Journal Ltd.)

Ardrey, Robert: *African Genesis* (Fontana, 1969)

Brittain, H. and Ripley, P. J. G.: *Simple History of East Africa* (Collins, 1963)

Carey, Margret: *Myths and Legends of Africa* (Hamlyn, 1970)

Cox, Thornton: *East Africa: Traveller's Guide* (Thornton Cox, 1973); *Southern Africa: Traveller's Guide* (Thornton Cox, 1975)

Expedition (international exploration and travel magazine) (World Expeditionary Association, 45 Brompton Road, London SW3)

Forbes, Rosita: *The Secret of the Sahara*

Fordham, Paul: *The Geography of African Affairs* (Penguin, 1974)

Hall, Richard: *Discovery of Africa* (Hamlyn, 1970)

Hallett, Jean-Pierre: *Animal Kitabu; Congo Kitabu* (Hamish Hamilton)

Hallett, R. H. (ed.): *The Niger Journal of Richard and John Lander* (Routledge, 1965)

Hemingway, Ernest: *The Green Hills of Africa* (Penguin, 1966)

Kingsnorth, G. W.: *Africa South of the Sahara* (C.U.P., 1962)

Legum, Colin: *Africa: A Handbook** (Penguin, 1969)

Moorehead, Alan: *The Blue Nile* (Hamish Hamilton, 1972); *The White Nile* (Penguin, 1973); *No Room in the Ark* (Penguin, 1970)

Oliver, Roland and Fage, J. D.: *A Short History of Africa* (Penguin, 1970)

Preservation of Personal Health in Warm Climates (Ross Institute of Tropical Hygiene: see p. 50)

Raven, Susan: *Rome in Africa* (Evans Bros., 1969)

Ricciardi, Mirella: *Vanishing Africa* (Collins, 1975)

Ruark, Robert: *Something of Value* (Corgi, 1970); *Uhuru* (Corgi, 1968)

Segal, Aaron and Allen, Phillip: *The Traveller's Africa* (Hopkinson Blake: N.Y.)

Seligman, C. G.: *Races of Africa* (O.U.P., 1966)

Stevens, Jon: *Sahara is Yours* (Constable, 1969)

Traveller's Guide to Africa (African Development, Wheatsheaf House, Carmelite Street, London EC4, 1975)

Wellard, J.: *The Great Sahara* (Hutchinson, 1964)

* It is highly recommended that a copy of *Africa: a Handbook* be obtained or read.

Part 2
Formalities

Chart I: Vehicle and Driving Documentation

R Required
NR Not required
NRA Not required
   advisable
NDL National
   driving licence
IDP International
   driving permit

	Carnet de passages	Vehicle registration book	Driving licence	Insurance 3rd party	Driving side road	Petrol coupons	Octane rating
ALGERIA	NR	R	IDP	R	Rt	YES	89–98
BOTSWANA	R	R	IDP	R	Lt		84–93
CAMEROUN	R	NRA	IDP		Rt		85–93
C.A.R.	R	NRA	IDP		Rt		85–93
DAHOMEY	R	NRA	IDP		Rt		83–87
EGYPT	R	NRA	IDP	R	Rt		86
GHANA	R	NRA	NDL	R	Rt		84–95
IVORY COAST	R	NRA	IDP		Rt		87–95
KENYA	R	NRA	NDL	R	Lt		83
LIBYA	R	NRA	NDL		Rt		99
MALAWI	R	NRA	NDL	R	Lt		83–93
MALI	R	NRA	IDP		Rt		89
MAURITANIA	R	NRA	IDP		Rt		96
MOROCCO	NR	R	NDL	R	Rt	YES	89–96
MOZAMBIQUE	R	NRA	IDP		Rt		82
NIGER	R	NRA	IDP		Rt		83–93
NIGERIA	R	NRA	IDP	R	Rt		83–95
RHODESIA	R	R	IDP	R	Lt		83–93
RWANDA	R	NRA	IDP		Rt		95
SENEGAL	R	NRA	IDP		Rt		87–95
SOUTH AFRICA	R	NRA	IDP	R	Lt		87–93
SP. SAHARA	R	NRA	IDP		Rt		96
SUDAN	R	NRA	IDP	R	Lt		80–95
TANZANIA	R	NRA	IDP	R	Lt		87
TCHAD	R	NRA	IDP		Rt		85–93
TOGOLAND	R	NRA	NDL		Rt		83–94
TUNISIA	NR	R	NDL	R	Rt		88
UGANDA	R	NRA	NDL	R	Lt		83–95
ZAIRE	R	NRA	IDP		Rt		93–95
ZAMBIA	R	NRA	NDL	R	Lt		87–95

Notes to Chart I
Customs

A Carnet de Passages en Douanes is required to enable a visitor temporarily to import a private motor vehicle into most countries outside Europe, and this the Royal Automobile Club will provide for travellers against a bank guarantee, or cash deposit, to cover possible customs duties. It is most important that the record of entry and exit for each country is recorded by the respective customs on the counterfoil of each page. It is the duty of the customs to make these endorsements but it is the vehicle owner's responsibility to see that it is carried out. It is not necessary to have a Carnet for a visit to Algeria only.

Although a Carnet de Passages en Douanes is not required for Nigeria, the High Commissioner will not issue a visa or entry permit unless a Carnet is presented at the time of application for a visa or entry permit.

The Carnet will not include Rhodesia. At the discretion of the Rhodesian customs officials at the place of entry into the country, motorists without a Carnet for Rhodesia may be allowed to obtain a customs temporary import permit for the vehicle without a deposit for customs duty.

New regulations have come into force concerning the entry into Zaire of foreign tourists and transit travellers with motor vehicles. All visitors must pass through Kinshasa and be cleared by customs there. Kinshasa can only be approached by river barge from Bangui or by ferry across the river from Brazzaville (Congo). Visitors may then proceed to Kisangani on similar transportation to exit on the prescribed routes mentioned on pages 179–180.

It is envisaged that the regulations will be relaxed towards the end of 1975, thus enabling overlanders to enter and exit the country on the normal routes.

Vehicle Insurance

The International Certificate of Motor Insurance (Green Card) is not valid beyond Morocco. Overlanders are therefore advised to contact their own insurance company for further assistance or information. It may not be mandatory to be in possession of a third-party insurance in some of the countries in Africa, but it is very unwise not to take out cover in case of an accident. The chart therefore indicates a requirement for third-party insurance in each country.

Insurance can generally be bought at the Moroccan, Algerian and Tunisian frontiers; it is not obtainable at the Mauritanian, Senegal, Gambian and Niger borders. Reports indicate that it is not asked for either. As it is not always possible to obtain insurance at the borders of the countries to be visited, travellers are advised to obtain cover before they start their journey.

International Certificate of Motor Vehicle

This is required for travelling through Nigeria. The certificate must be presented to the provincial police headquarters on arrival in the country for stamping and for the issue of a circulation permit.

Permission to motor through the Sudan

Formal permission is essential, and applications should be made in sufficient time for them to be sent to Khartoum and be returned to the applicant before his departure from the United Kingdom or country of residence. The forms should be sent to one of the following authorities:

Sudan Embassy or Legation in country of residence

Permanent Under Secretary, Ministry of Interior, Khartoum
Permits normally take from four to six weeks to process, and are despatched by air. The form of application is given in Appendix I (pages 229–232).

International Driving Permit

The Royal Automobile Club will issue an International Driving Permit to any person over the age of 18 years who is domiciled in the United Kingdom and in possession of a valid British driving licence.

Notes to Chart II
Health Regulations

Visitors must possess valid international certificates of vaccination against smallpox, cholera and yellow-fever, which should be dated at least 10 days before the date of departure. Whilst not essential, vaccinations for TABT (typhoid, para typhoid and tetanus) are recommended. Malaria is prevalent in many regions and visitors are advised to carry a supply of one of the anti-malaria drugs.

Overlanders may be refused entry into a country or be subjected to a period of quarantine if they are not in possession of the necessary health certificates. Certain innoculations may not be required in some countries, but it is advisable to have all those listed in Chart II if you intend to travel in Africa or onwards to Australia.

As the local requirements for innoculations are subject to change at short notice, you are advised to enquire which innoculations are needed before you begin your journey.

Medical Insurance

You are advised to take out adequate insurance for medical or hospital treatment in case of illness or an accident. Hospital accommodation and consultants' fees are very expensive throughout the African continent. An insurance broker or the Royal Automobile Club would advise you on adequate world wide cover.

Chart II: Health Regulations

R Required NR Not required NRA Not required advisable	Smallpox	Cholera	Yellow fever	Typhoid Para typhoid Tetanus	Malaria
ALGERIA	R	R	—	NRA	YES
BOTSWANA	R	R	—	NRA	YES
CAMEROUN	R	R	R	NRA	YES
C.A.R.	R	R	R	NRA	YES
DAHOMEY	R	R	R	NRA	YES
EGYPT	R	R	—	R	YES
GHANA	R	R	R	NRA	YES
IVORY COAST	R	R	R	NRA	YES
KENYA	R	R	R	NRA	YES
LIBYA	R	R	—	R	—
MALAWI	R	R	R	NRA	YES
MALI	R	R	R	NRA	YES
MAURITANIA	R	R	R	NRA	YES
MOROCCO	R	R	—	NRA	YES
MOZAMBIQUE	R	R	R	NRA	YES
NIGER	R	R	R	NRA	YES
NIGERIA	R	R	R	NRA	YES
RHODESIA	R	R	R	NRA	YES
RWANDA	R	R	R	NRA	YES
SENEGAL	R	R	R	NRA	YES
SOUTH AFRICA	R	R	R	NRA	YES
SPANISH SAHARA	R	R	R	NRA	YES
SUDAN	R	R	R	NRA	YES
TANZANIA	R	R	R	NRA	YES
TCHAD	R	R	R	NRA	YES
TOGOLAND	R	R	R	NRA	YES
TUNISIA	R	R	—	NRA	YES
UGANDA	R	R	R	NRA	YES
ZAIRE	R	R	R	NRA	YES
ZAMBIA	R	R	R	NRA	YES

Chart III: Visa Requirements

	British	Irish	Australian	Canadian	New Zealand	American
V: Visa VP: Visitor's pass EP: Entry permit NR: None required						
ALGERIA	NR	NR	V	V	V	V
BOTSWANA	NR	NR	NR	NR	NR	NR
CAMEROUN	NR	NR	NR	NR	NR	NR
C.A.R.	V	V	V	V	V	V
DAHOMEY	V	V	V	V	V	V
EGYPT	EP	EP	EP	EP	EP	EP
GHANA	EP	V	EP	EP	EP	V
IVORY COAST	NR	NR	V	V	V	V
KENYA	EP	EP	EP	EP	EP	V
LIBYA	V	V	V	V	V	V
MALAWI	NR	NR	NR	NR	NR	NR
MALI	V	V	V	V	V	V
MAURITANIA	V	V	V	V	V	V
MOROCCO	NR	NR	NR	NR	NR	NR
MOZAMBIQUE	NR	NR	NR	NR	V	NR
NIGER	V	V	V	V	V	V
NIGERIA	EP	EP	EP	EP	EP	EP
RHODESIA	NR	NR	NR	NR	NR	NR
RWANDA	V	V	V	V	V	V
SENEGAL	V	V	V	V	V	V
SOUTH AFRICA	NR	NR	V	NR	V	V
SP. SAHARA	V	V	V	V	V	V
SUDAN	V	V	V	V	V	V
TANZANIA	VP	NR	VP	VP	VP	V
TCHAD	V	V	V	V	V	V
TOGO	V	V	V	V	V	V
TUNISIA	NR	NR	V	V	NR	NR
UGANDA	V	V	V	V	V	V
ZAIRE	V	V	V	V	V	V
ZAMBIA	NR	NR	NR	NR	NR	V

Notes to Chart III
Visas

These are required for most of the countries to be visited, and should be obtained before the start of the journey. Holders of British passports must obtain entry permits for Commonwealth countries, and these should always be obtained before leaving the United Kingdom. Enquiries should always be made at the Embassies, Consulates and High Commissions of the countries being visited, regarding visa requirements, health certificates, entry and visitor's regulations, etc. An early approach to the appropriate authorities is to be recommended, as certain health regulations may need to be observed, and any application may have to be referred to the capital of the country concerned.

Requests for visas to visit Zaire must be made in sufficient time for the Embassy to telex full details of the persons travelling to Kinshasa. Two weeks at least should be allowed for a reply.

As a result of regulations issued by the Libyan government, the Libyan Embassy in London will only issue visas for Libya if the applicant's particulars are written in the Arabic language.

British, Canadian and Irish citizens who are not of 'pure European descent' must obtain visas for entry into South Africa.

Note: As travel regulations are liable to change at short notice, travellers are advised to check on the regulations in force at the time they intend to travel. British passport holders should approach the Passport Office, Clive House, Petty France, London SW1 (tel: 01-222 8010).

Part 3
Equipment

Vehicle

This is the most important piece of equipment you will be taking with you, and you should realize from the start that motoring on desert tracks calls for robust vehicles in perfect mechanical condition. This cannot be emphasized too strongly. A four-wheel type is strongly advised, and in some areas would be vital. The engine should be sufficiently powerful to cope with the extremely difficult conditions that will be met. The vehicle should possess adequate ground clearance, and this factor will rule out certain saloon types. You should also take into account the height and weight limits likely to be encountered on boats, bridges, etc. It should obviously be sufficiently roomy to take passengers and all your gear in comfort – and remember that it should never be loaded beyond 75 per cent of the manufacturer's recommended limit. A list of suitable vehicles – with details of their respective rates of fuel consumption – is given on page 25.

The vehicle should be capable of carrying additional fuel to ensure that it has a range of 700–800 miles. It is advisable to have an extra fuel tank fitted, as jerry cans create a storage and multiple evaporation problem, and can also be very dangerous. Remember that a high rate of evaporation will take place because of the extreme heat: with this in mind, you should ensure that the spare fuel capacity is not less than 25 per cent of the total required to cover the distance between known refuelling points, when driving under adverse conditions.

It is also advisable to have a dual pump/filter system fitted, in case of sand blocking the feed to the engine. If possible, an oil-bath type filter for the carburettor should be used, and this will need to be cleaned daily.

If you intend to buy or hire a vehicle specifically for the journey, you will be faced with the choice between petrol or diesel. Briefly, the advantages of the petrol engine are that it has a high power and torque output and a higher maximum speed than the diesel engine. It is quieter and cleaner, and more easily understood – this is a definite advantage if you think you will be needing outside mechanical help. The likelihood of obtaining spares in Africa is also far higher than with diesel engines. The diesel engine has no ignition system, which is an advantage when wading shallow streams and rivers. It is cheaper, and the fuel consumption is better than

A fully equipped Land Rover on the first stage of its trans-African journey – on a desert track between In Salah and Tamanrasset, Algeria.

that of a petrol engine. It also carries less risk of fire. On balance, although the petrol engine is more expensive to run, the question of spares and repairs probably make it a better bet.

The most suitable vehicle in all respects is the Land Rover, especially if it is fitted out as a motor caravan. U.K. residents can obtain expert advice on motor caravans from Mr Tony Wilson, who will also arrange their purchase or hire for trans-continental travellers. He has travelled extensively with motor caravans, and was a successful competitor in the gruelling London to Sydney marathon. He is available at Northcroft, Dulwich Common, London SE21 7HJ, tel: 01-693 7379.

Regulations require a nationality plate to be fixed to the rear of any vehicle or trailer, as near as possible to the registration plate. The letters should be in capital Latin characters, having a minimum height of 3.1 ins and width of 0.4 ins, printed in black on a white oval. The minimum dimensions of the oval should be 6.9 ins in width and 4.5 ins in height. A self-adhesive G.B. plate can be supplied by the Royal Automobile Club.

Motor cycles are not suitable for trans-African journeys, and in some areas are strictly prohibited.

Caravans and Trailers

It is possible to tow caravans and trailers on most of the main highways in Morocco and Algeria, along the coastal route to Egypt, and on the major highways in East and South Africa. Before deciding to take a caravan or trailer with you, however, you should first study the gradients of the roads you will be taking, to ensure that they are suitable.

Caravans cannot be towed across Africa, due to the difficult terrain in the Southern Sahara and the earth roads in Central Africa – and in fact they are strictly prohibited in the Saharan deep south. A light trailer can sometimes be towed behind a Land Rover, but this is not advisable as the risk of breakdown and of losing the trailer is very high.

Spare Parts and Tools

You are advised to take a maintenance handbook and workshop manual for your vehicle; in addition, a practical knowledge of car servicing and repairs is invaluable. Service stations and garages can quite often be few and far between, and in some areas only primitive facilities are available.

When selecting spare parts, you should pay special attention to the particular weaknesses of your vehicle. Once inside Africa, spare parts may well prove unobtainable, and long delays can be caused by having them sent over great distances. Usually, most vehicle manufacturers will recommend an adequate stock for long-distance travel.

As a general rule, the following spares should always be carried:

> fan belt
> sparking plugs
> distributor contact set
> condenser
> light bulbs
> two spare wheels
> two spare tyres and tubes*

petrol pump
four oil filters
radiator hose and assorted hoses
rotor arm
HT lead
fuses
starter brushes
dynamo brushes
distributor cap
ignition coil
fuel pump repair kit
by-pass hose
carburettor repair kit
* Note: tubeless tyres should not be used on a trans-African journey; new tyres are essential, radials if possible.

A comprehensive tool kit is essential, and should include the following:

two hydraulic jacks (minimum lift 12 ins)
wheel brace
tyre pump
tyre pressure gauge
puncture outfit
tyre levers
wire, including insulated wire
insulating tape
box of assorted nuts, bolts, screws and split pins
strong tow rope and block and tackle
torch and spare batteries
warning triangle (see page 77)

Emergency Equipment

The practical hazards of a trans-African journey should not be underestimated. At some time your vehicle will inevitably become stuck in soft sand or mud; in the equatorial regions such as Zaire (Congo), fallen trees or broken-down vehicles may force you to leave the main track and cut your way through the adjacent bush

Carrying out bridge repairs before crossing, on the way to Titule, Zaire.

or forest; makeshift bridges will often need additional support before you can cross in safety, and on some rivers you may have to construct your own ferry out of a combination of planks and dugout canoes. Thus it is vital that you take suitable equipment for extricating yourself and your vehicle from such 'emergencies'.

The ideal solution to many of these problems is the Pierced Steel Plank (PSP), originally used for laying emergency airfields and roads. Each plank, measuring 10 ft × 15 ins, is grooved, with the edges of the perforations sunk, ensuring the highest possible rigidity. PSP can be used in soft sand or mud to provide the driving wheels with the necessary grip to get the vehicle out, and are invaluable for filling in gaps in makeshift bridges. They can be obtained from Tent and Tarpaulin Ltd., 101–3 Brixton Hill, London SW2, tel: 01-674 0121/3.

You should carry the following 'emergency' equipment with you at all times (although additional to normal requirements, it should not be considered an optional extra!):

at least two Pierced Steel Planks or two 6–8 ft aluminium ladders
short handled shovels for clearing sand, etc.

two strong flat bases for the jacks
machetes, axes or saws
some good strong lengths of rope

Survival Equipment

However well you prepare for your trans-African journey, there is always the possibility that you and your vehicle will become stranded in an extremely remote area. Reserves of fuel and water—both for yourself and for your vehicle—are essential, and should be kept topped up at all times. In addition, you should have adequate means of signalling your plight in the case of a complete breakdown.
    The following should always be carried:

    reserve stocks of water, including distilled water, for vehicle lubricants
    25 per cent reserve of petrol
    two days' reserve of food
    $2\frac{1}{2}$ gallon reserve per person of drinking water
    plastic sheet for collecting dew at night
    mirror
    white sheet
    two smoke bombs or flares (one black, one red) for signalling to aircraft

Smoke bombs, flares, candles and rockets etc. can be obtained from Pain-Wessex Ltd., High Post, Salisbury, Wilts., or from a ship's chandler.

Navigation Equipment

It is most important that you keep a log during a trans-African journey, especially when crossing the Sahara. In order to note time, distance, direction, important features etc., you should be equipped with the following:

graph paper
protractor
ruler
dividers
a good compass
a pair of binoculars (for recognizing desert track navigational aids)

A new navigating device called the 'Cruiserfix' is now available, which, it is claimed, will fix your position within a few miles anywhere on land, sea, or in the air. This device takes advantage of the fact that the difference between the sun time at Greenwich and the sun time anywhere else is proportional to the difference in longitude between the two places. It embodies a simple sun clock with which to intercept the Local Apparent Time directly from the sun's shadow. When the LAT has been corrected (by adding or subtracting a few minutes) to Local Mean Time, the LMT is compared with GMT to find the difference. The observer's time meridian is then disclosed and the longitude can be found by equating four minutes of time to one degree of arc. Since the sun clock has to be rectified to suit the observer's latitude, the 'Cruiserfix' automatically enables one to calculate the noon latitude. Declination is dealt with mechanically, by simply setting the instrument to the correct date. The diurnal error of the sun (which does not keep regular time) is provided by extracting the day's error from the graph.

Use of this instrument requires only a knowledge of simple compass work. It has only to be aligned to true south or north, according to hemisphere. Obviously, a device of this simple kind cannot be expected to give a pin-point position, but results indicate that with care and a little practice it will fix the observer's meridian to within about 5 nautical mls and latitude to within about 15 mls. It takes about 30 seconds to get a latitude and about 90 seconds to get a longitude. It can also be used as a sun compass for course keeping, if required.

The 'Cruiserfix' can be obtained from Navigemus (IoM) Ltd., Great Downs, Tollesbury, Essex, and costs £5.18 including VAT. It is self-contained and provides all the necessary ephemeris. Folded flat, it will stow into a jacket pocket.

In addition, you should obviously be equipped with a good selection of detailed maps, covering all the countries through which you intend to travel. The finest maps of any scale can be supplied by the Royal Automobile Club and a price list giving the complete range is obtainable from them on request.

The recommended maps for overlanders are Michelin Nos. 153, 154, 155, 169, 172, 175.

First Aid Kit

The following items should be taken, as a minimum. All first-aid articles are extremely expensive to buy in Africa, so it is sensible to take a generous stock with you.

> Paludrine, or any one of the recommended anti-malarian drugs
> tourniquet
> lancet
> scissors
> sticking plaster
> Mercurochrome or other germicide
> hydrogen peroxide
> antibiotic cream
> vaccines against scorpion and snake bites (these can be obtained from the Pasteur Institute, Algiers)
> an analgesic
> three compressed dressings
> two rolls of stretch bandages
> aspirin or similar tablets

The booklet *Preservation of Personal Health in Warm Climates*, published by the Ross Institute of Tropical Hygiene, is an essential companion for overlanders. It is obtainable, price 50p, from the London School of Hygiene and Tropical Medicine, Keppel Street, London WC1E 7HT.

To avoid any misunderstanding, you should keep all medicines, etc. in their proprietary packs. Zeal in stamping out illegal drug trafficking has been known to express itself in chemical analysis of talcum powder or aspirin tablets – a lengthy, expensive procedure best avoided! (See also page 64.)

Security

Hints on safeguarding your own personal security and the security of your possessions are given on page 75. Before setting out on your journey, however, you should ensure that your vehicle is fitted with adequate security devices.

Locks should be fitted to secure all moveable equipment stowed on the outside of the vehicle. This should include the spare wheel and the petrol filler cap.

An anti-burglar alarm should be fitted–the louder the better, especially if the note is one that will cause surprise.

A strongbox should be fitted out of sight somewhere inside the vehicle, for storing all your valuables at night.

If your vehicle has a soft top–as is the case with some Land Rovers–it is advisable to have a metal framework fitted underneath the canvas, for added security.

Camping Equipment

Camping equipment suitable for your needs is obtainable from good camping equipment stockists and military surplus stores. In London, two recommended outlets are:

Tent and Tarpaulin Ltd.,
101–3 Brixton Hill, London SW2
Tel. 01–674 0121/3

Expedition Supplies,
280 Old Brompton Road, London SW5
Tel. 01–370 6677

Both companies have experience in fitting out expeditions.

Camping gear in general needs no elaboration, but you are advised to study the following hints.

A pair of sleeping-bag sheets should be taken, so that you always have one clean and ready for use. They can easily be made by sewing together a large sheet.

51

Making camp by the roadside in the forests of Zaire.

A warm sleeping bag is essential if you intend to cross the Sahara.

Mosquito nets are essential if you intend to do any camping at all. In addition, to reduce the nuisance of flying insects in the evening, buy a double-bed mosquito net–either before you set out, or on arrival at Algiers or Kano. It should have an extra skirt sewn on to it to provide extra height. Used as a lean-to, attached to the top of the vehicle and supported by two tent poles, it provides an ideal covered area to sit in when in camp at night.

Gas for cooking stoves is not available between Algeria and Kenya; you should therefore take 'back-up' cooking equipment which uses petrol or paraffin.

Some means of purifying water is essential when travelling in Africa. (See also page 77.) Chlorine or other such water-sterilisation tablets are useful for washing vegetables and fresh fruit, and for use in bulk water supplies for personal washing facilities. They can be obtained from most chemist's shops, and it is sensible to buy a generous supply before starting your journey. But for drinking water, the only really satisfactory way of removing all chlorine, bacteria and dirt–without affecting the natural mineral content of the water–is to put it through a water purification system. The latest development (originating in the U.S.A.) is a small compact unit which fits easily under or over a sink unit. It contains a flexible cartridge which cannot be broken and is capable of filtering some ten times finer than those units previously available. It can be very easily coupled to an existing pressurised water supply system, or is available with a built-in hand pump which makes it self-contained. As one needs to purify water only for actual consumption, the self-contained unit is advisable, as opposed to one that is totally dependent on the pressure system. The cartridges are disposable and stop the flow of water automatically when exhausted, making the need for replacement self-evident. Cartridges are available for quantities of up to 450 gallons, and only take a few minutes to replace. They are guaranteed to remove all active solids, algae, dirt, rust and scale, and to provide completely safe, pure, fresh drinking water from virtually any non-salt water source. Several models are available, from a small plastic pocket unit at under £5, to the one-gallon-per-minute domestic/commercial unit for plumbing in. The suppliers are Safari (Water Treatments) Ltd., 28 The Spain, Petersfield, Hampshire, tel. Petersfield 4452. They will be pleased to send full details on request, together with copies of laboratory reports.

The International Camping Carnet is an invaluable aid to successful camping. This is issued by the Fédération Internationale de l'Automobile, a world-wide international organisation whose members include the Royal Automobile Club and automobile clubs of over seventy nations. Besides acting as an identity document and as evidence that the holder is a responsible camper/caravanner, the Carnet allows entry to sites belonging to other international organisations, sometimes at a reduced rate. Over and above this, the Carnet contains an insurance policy covering third-party risks while camping or caravanning, providing the party is travelling together and the Carnet bears the stamp of the current year.

The application form for a Camping Carnet must be completed accurately in all respects. (Forms can be obtained from the Royal Automobile Club.) A Carnet may be issued without a photograph, but it is strongly recommended that one is inserted into the document. Should you be asked to leave your passport with the camp-site proprietor during your stay at a camp site (other than for registration purposes), the Carnet will normally be accepted as an alternative security document – providing it carries a photograph.

Clothing

Because of the extreme variations in climate of the countries to be traversed, you should take both lightweight and warm clothing. It should be tough, practical, and suitable for all occasions. You may find the following hints useful.

Some woollen clothing (pullovers, scarves, etc.) should be carried for the chilly evenings and mornings between October and April. This is especially important if you intend to cross the Sahara, where the temperature at night can be very low.

You should take sunglasses and a wide-brimmed hat to give protection from the sun. Again, if you intend to cross the Sahara, you should have a 'cheche' – the muslin veil Saharans use to protect their heads – to give cover against the sirocco and sandstorms. These can be bought in Algiers.

Synthetic fabrics, such as nylon, should be avoided. Fabrics made of a mixture of artifical fibre and cotton are more suitable, and more easily washed.

Be prepared for biting mosquitoes! It is best to wear long-sleeved shirts and trousers at night; ankle-length boots are also very practical in this respect.

The customs and laws of certain states will impose certain limitations on the clothing you take (see also page 62). Women in mini-skirts are liable to be arrested, and in some states women are not allowed to wear trousers or shorts. Lady visitors should take skirts or dresses which will cover the knees when in an upright position. In Malawi, it is an offence for men to wear bell-bottomed trousers. Under the Decency of Dress (Amendment) Act 1974, these are defined as 'any flared trousers so made that the circumference of each leg thereof measured along the bottom edge is greater than six-fifths of the circumference of such leg measured at its narrowest point parallel to the aforesaid bottom edge'. It is best to play safe and take trousers that fall well within the legal definition.

Personal Effects

Remember that the weight factor is very important, and all too easily abused, when it comes to personal equipment and effects: overloading a vehicle is often the cause of mechanical breakdown or poor performance over difficult roads.

You may find the following hints useful.

It is advisable to take cleansing creams for removing the dust from your skin; to counteract the dry hot climate of the Sahara you will also need moisturising face-creams and vaseline for the lips. These are all most expensive to buy en route. By the same token, ladies should take a good supply of the cosmetics they will need.

An assortment of different sizes of plastic containers and bags is invaluable for carrying personal effects.

Camera film is expensive and difficult to obtain in some parts of Africa. It is wise to take more than you think you may need. You should also take a suitable container for keeping your camera and films cool and dry (see also page 74).

A small supply of passport photographs will come in handy and forestall possible delays when these are required for special permits, etc.

All members of your party should carry a card giving their blood group, and details of any allergies or diet instructions. This can save valuable time in case of an emergency.

Part 4
Practical Hints for Overlanders

Alcoholic Beverages

All the countries you will be passing through impose heavy penalties upon persons found driving whilst under the influence of drink; you are liable to be heavily fined, imprisoned, or both.

Breaking Down

If you break down, you should immediately consult your journey log (see page 73) together with the relevant map and route itinerary, in order to establish a fix or position. You should then enter the details in your log, together with an appreciation of the situation.

In desert and uninhabited areas, you should always stay with the vehicle and wait for a fellow traveller to come along. You

In the event of a breakdown, you should always remain with your vehicle . . . The result of running into a hidden rut after a rainstorm, on the road between Isio and Mongbere, Zaire.

can then enlist his help, or at least request him to carry a message to the nearest place of habitation–preferably one that you have just left and where you have details, names, etc., of those who can help you. Naturally, any decision you may make will have to take into consideration the distances involved; those travelling in the opposite direction to your own party may well be able to supply you with useful advice and information on what lies ahead. Whatever you do, you should make sure that the nearest police post is informed of your plight.

In an extreme emergency, a flare sent up whilst an aircraft is overhead will indicate that help is urgently needed. Petrol poured over a tyre and set alight will also provide sufficient smoke to attract attention. If available, white sheets should also be spread out on the ground. Signals of this nature are noticed and reported; however, do not expect swift action and conserve all vital supplies of water and food for as long as you can.

Camping

Camping facilities in Africa have yet to be developed and sites are generally only available near the larger towns and in game reserves. Nevertheless it is possible to camp in most places, though great care should be taken in choosing a site.

The following simple rules should be observed when camping.

Use designated camp sites whenever possible.

Always request permission in inhabited areas, as a matter of courtesy.

Camp away from oases and villages if you wish to avoid flies, but remember that it is sometimes wiser to camp within the protective limits of a village, preferably near to a police post or to some official body.

Do not camp on low ground close to a river or in a dry stream bed. There is always the danger of a flash flood.

Camping in game parks and reserves is not allowed except at the designated sites, where a fee is charged.

Rest houses are situated throughout all the former British-administered territories. Whilst prior permission must always be obtained to use them, camping may be allowed within their grounds on arrival, thus eliminating curious villagers who are apt to prove

Beware of flash floods – the consequence, on the track between Aderbis-sinat and Tanout, Niger.

a trial when camping in the open. Religious missions, too, may provide the same facilities.

Daily Routine

The day's journey should begin at day-break and continue to 10.00 hrs, when a stop of one or two hours is made for 'brunch'. Thereafter, halts should be made every hour for a few minutes' rest. Driving should continue through the middle of the day until 15.30 hrs, when a suitable camp site should be located. It is advisable to be camped by 16.00 hrs: this gives sufficient time for a vehicle check, establishing the camp and cooking the main meal of the day. Everything should then be cleared away before nightfall: in the southern and central regions, this comes suddenly, at about 18.30 hrs. It is never wise to make camp in the dark, as equipment gets lost, and insects become a nuisance, being attracted by lights in the camp.

Dress and Appearance

Hints on the type of clothing most suitable for an overland journey are given on page 54. You should also take pains to ensure that your general appearance conforms to the conventions of the countries you will be travelling through. Some of the developing states are highly critical of Europeans' appearance and apparel in general. Apart from giving offence, travellers who ignore such conventions may find themselves liable to prosecution. You should make sure that you are modestly dressed at all times. Also remember that men with beards or long hair are treated with suspicion, as they are very difficult to identify.

Under Malawian law, it is an offence for men to wear bell-bottomed trousers (see page 54 for definition) or to have long hair: hair should not fall below an imaginary line drawn horizontally around the head at the level of the mouth. In public places, it is illegal for women to expose any part of their bodies or undergarments (i.e. including stockings and tights but not including any underskirt that is not transparent) between the lower level of the kneecaps and the waist. Furthermore, it is illegal for women to wear trousers or shorts. Visitors to Malawi who contravene the law in these respects are liable to be refused entry by the immigration authorities or, if they are within Malawi's borders, to be arrested and prosecuted.

The limitations on women's clothing do not apply when the wearer is within Blantyre or Lilongwe Airport, the Lakeshore hotels, or various designated national parks and forest reserves. It should be noted that they do apply, however, within hotels situated in the main towns and when in transit to any of the exempt areas. Certain exemptions are also made when the wearer is engaged in any form of sport for which such clothing is customary or if it is part of a national dress (such as in the Asian community).

Driving in Mud

This calls for a similar technique to driving in sand. Try not to stop: if you do, a push start is advised with a mat, cut brush

Negotiating a badly rutted earth road after the rains, between Bambili and Barambo, Zaire.

or loose stones placed ahead and if possible under the driving wheels. To achieve the latter, the wheels may have to be jacked up. Great care must be taken if the vehicle's wheels slip into another set of tracks: never turn the front wheels more than necessary, and get out of these tracks as soon as you can.

Driving in Sand

Soft sandy sections should not be rushed: a reconnaissance ahead on foot is always worthwhile and may save a lot of wasted time. You should proceed forward slowly, preferably in second gear, keeping the engine revolutions down. The wheels must never be allowed to spin, as this will cause the vehicle to sink rapidly–ending up in a position from which it can only be extricated with a great deal of time and energy.

Typical corrugations on a desert track near In Amguel, north of Tamanrasset, Algeria.

When approaching long stretches of loose sand, always reduce tyre pressures, as this will provide the vehicle with better flotation. The tyres should be re-inflated as soon as you reach harder ground.

Sand mats, ladders or–best of all–Pierced Steel Planks are the best aids for keeping a vehicle moving over soft sandy ground. If your vehicle should become stuck, it is advisable to adopt the following routine immediately: jack up wheels by using two jacks if possible–remember that the jacks themselves may need some support in order to stop them from sinking straight into the sand–fill in holes made by the wheels–place mat, ladder or PSP under wheels–wind down jacks and remove–start engine and engage second gear–drive forward keeping engine revolutions down as much as possible.

Drugs

All of the countries you will be visiting impose very severe penalties for the possession of narcotic drugs. Whichever route you take, you will pass through numerous check points where your vehicle is liable to be stopped and searched by the police (see also page 75).

In all cases, the owner of the vehicle is responsible if narcotic drugs are found in the possession of any of the passengers. He will be charged for possession whether he had any prior knowledge of such drug carrying or not.

Ferries

Ferries of one kind or another are available to cross the rivers on all of the major routes. Because of their diversity you must expect to participate at some time in their operation. Motorized ferries need batteries to start the engine and you will be asked to supply one; sometimes two are needed and delays can occur in waiting for another traveller to come along to supply the extra one.

Loading on to the improvised dugout-canoe ferry between Bangui, C.A.R. and Zongo, Zaire.

There are basically three types of ferries: motor barges with flat or well decks, rafts operated by ropes and pulleys, and dugout canoes fastened together with wooden planks to form a platform for the vehicle. The motive power for this latter type of ferry is generally native paddlers who expect to be paid for their services. Ferries are normally free but one is often asked to pay.

Game Parks and Reserves

All regulations and movement orders must be strictly obeyed. Speed limits vary between 20 to 30 mph. Vehicles must only be dismounted at the places so designated (this rule also applies to camping, which is generally in the vicinity of game lodges). Movement is only allowed between dawn and dusk – vehicles must not be moved at night. A fee is charged per person for visits to the parks and for camping.

Health

Because of the climatic and environmental conditions, many health hazards face the African or desert traveller. Five important ones are:

Heat Disorders: Extreme heat can cause conditions of heat exhaustion or, more severely, heat stroke, if the body is not adequately supplied with fluids and salt. During the hot season it is essential to drink as much 'safe' liquid as indicated by thirst, together with about the equivalent of one teaspoonful of salt daily in the diet. 'Safe' fluids include boiled water, bottled mineral water, or failing these, tea without milk. Milk should always be boiled.

Intestinal Disorders: These include the dysenteries and all the associated diarrhoeal disorders caused principally by eating bacterially contaminated or highly irritating foodstuffs. A good working rule is to eat simple, recently prepared food which, if cooked, should be thoroughly cooked. Avoid food concoctions whose preparation necessitates frequent handling, for example, sausages, kebabs and

Tim Bailey meets a friendly visitor to his camp in the Tzavo National Park, Kenya.

meat pastes. Bazaar ice should never be put into drinks. All unpeelable fruit and vegetables should be washed in boiled water. To eat exposed food from an open bazaar shop or stall without further cooking is to ask for trouble.

Bilharzia: This is a disease obtained by drinking, washing, wading or swimming in rivers, lakes or dams containing a minute water snail carrying the infection. Large areas of North and Central Africa are affected by Bilharzia: great care should be taken and local enquiries should always be made.

Malaria: Whilst all mosquitoes do not carry malaria, the malarial mosquito is prevalent throughout the whole of Africa. Precautions must be taken: mosquito nets should always be used at night, and one of the recommended prophylactic drugs should be taken regularly.

Hookworm: Damp ground near water in villages is invariably infested with larvae hookworm, a debilitating parasite of the human body which works its way in through the soles of the feet. To avoid the hookworm, never walk barefoot on damp ground.

Hitch-hikers

Many of the travellers to and from Africa today have no visible means of support and rely solely upon the motorist for transportation. Whether you give lifts to hitch-hikers or not is a purely personal decision. However, you should be aware that any stranger represents a threat to your security, and that there is always the possibility that a hitch-hiker may be carrying drugs without your knowledge (see page 64).

Hospitals

In the large cities there are good hospitals; however, there is a huge demand for their services and treatment is likely to be somewhat impersonal and expensive. The food, usually vegetarian, is seldom palatable to the European. Private hospitals are available but charges are very high.

A typical government Rest House, built on a hill top overlooking savanna countryside, Nigeria.

Hotel accommodation

Suitable hotel accommodation can be found in all major towns. There are also a number of rest houses available on the main routes.

Accommodation between towns is limited and may not be to European standard. You should therefore plan your journey between towns accordingly.

Language

English and French are understood in all the larger towns you are likely to pass through. English is still widely used in those countries influenced by us in the past, and travellers should find little difficulty in being understood, except maybe in the country areas.

A : Arabic   P : Portuguese

E : English   S : Spanish

F : French

Algeria	F/A	Niger	F
Botswana	E	Nigeria	E
Cameroun	F	Rhodesia	E
C.A.R.	F	Rwanda	F
Dahomey	F	Senegal	F
Egypt	F/E/A	South Africa	E
Ghana	E	Spanish Sahara	S/A
Ivory Coast	F	Sudan	E/A
Kenya	E	Tanzania	E
Libya	A	Tchad	F
Malawi	E	Togo	F
Mali	F	Tunisia	F/A
Mauritania	F	Uganda	E
Morocco	F/A	Zaire	F
Mozambique	P	Zambia	E

Local Customs

Because of the diversity of the peoples in Africa, local customs vary greatly. You are advised to learn as much as you can from the many books available on the subject in public libraries (see reading list, page 29). Free literature is also generally available from the national tourist offices of the countries concerned.

Africans are by nature a friendly people, ever ready to help and to give information. You may sometimes become exasperated by minor officials, who, it must be remembered, are carrying out their duties across a barrier of language and culture. In such an event, courtesy, patience and a sense of humour will achieve far more than letting off steam. It is always unwise to force an official into a position from which retreat will mean loss of face.

Mail

'Poste Restante' services exist at large post offices, but mail for travellers should only be sent to places serviced by an International Airport. Kano, Nairobi, Lusaka and Johannesburg are recommended, places between them are not.

Minefields

In recent times, the emergence of new independent countries and the ensuing political struggles have in certain cases caused disputes between neighbouring countries. Borders are in dispute from time to time – those of Morocco, Algeria and Tunisia have been no exception. Civilians as well as soldiers have laid minefields, although these have now mostly been lifted or otherwise cleared. Nevertheless, the general terrain of these countries makes the positive clearing of minefields difficult, and casualties have been inflicted on those who have ignored the danger. To ensure complete safety, you should therefore only cross borders at the recognised crossing points.

Mosquitoes

Mosquitoes and other flying insects can be an intolerable nuisance in camp, as well as presenting a serious health hazard. Despite the heat, it is sensible to wear long-sleeved shirts and long trousers, keeping your arms and legs covered.

A mosquito-net awning, attached to the top of the vehicle and supported by two tent poles (see page 52) makes an ideal covered area to sit in when in camp at night. The lamp used to provide illumination should be hung somewhere safe outside the net. A basin with a little water in it, placed on the ground underneath the lamp, should catch insects that burn their wings on the lamp or are attracted by the reflected light on the water.

Navigation

Whilst map reading may be a simple matter for the experienced traveller, it becomes a very demanding and necessary task in the desert or in other uninhabited areas. It should be carried out with the utmost care and attention to detail. You should not always assume you are right or that you have correctly identified this or that place as the one on the map. You must make sure.

All the desert tracks are marked by some form of beacon, positioned in line of sight generally 2 or 3 km apart. These markers are usually cairns of stones, empty 40-gallon drums (sometimes with posts stuck in them), or Berliet-type markers (poles with rectangular plates on top). This latter type of marker is common, as they were put in by the French army.

A simple method of navigation is by Dead Reckoning: for example, if you travel due east for one mile, due south for one mile, due west for one mile, and due north for one mile, you should return to your original position. This is Dead Reckoning navigation in its simplest form. Although, obviously, it will only be completely

The featureless desert south of Tamanrasset, Algeria—look for the hard ground and choose your own route.

accurate on straight roads and tracks – a somewhat rare phenomenon in Africa! – it is a useful method and one that is fairly simple to operate.

The prerequisite for successful navigation of any kind is a detailed and up-to-date log of your journey – this cannot be over-emphasised. You should include the following details, at the very least:

> Mileage recorded on the milometer at the start point of the day's journey, on the hour, half-hour or quarter-hour depending on the terrain, at all stopping points, recognisable features (camp sites, etc.) and places where back-up facilities (water, petrol, food, etc.) are available.
> Driving times between all these points.
> Any bearings taken with a magnetic compass (see below).
> Notes and positions of other tracks leading into or away from the main track.
> Prominent hills or other geographical features (a sketch will help if you are unable to identify these immediately).
> Wells and other landmarks.
> General notes on the type and condition of the road or track.
> Names and addresses of garages and places where welding facilities are available; any 'useful' experiences: this information will be of enormous value should your vehicle break down (see also page 59).

By diligently entering all these facts into your log, you should be able to plot your position on the map. Additionally, if you have any cause for uncertainty, you should be able to 'back track' by back plotting the same information to your last known position (graph paper can be used for this).

When taking bearings with a magnetic compass, you should stand at least 30 yards away from your vehicle so as to be outside its magnetic field. Check that you have no metal substance on your person, as this may cause interference. It is important, too, to note any local magnetic variation.

Details of the 'Cruiserfix' navigating device are given on page 49. Remember that deviation has to be taken into account with this instrument as well – compass sights should consequently be taken well away from the magnetic field of your vehicle. You should also remember that an instrument of this simple kind cannot be expected to give a pin-point position: you should therefore take not less than three, and preferably five or six readings for any one position. The 'Cruiserfix' can also be used as a sun compass for course keeping, if required. If by misadventure the GMT is lost, it can be calculated from any location whose bearings are known: simply find the LMT and set off the longitude difference between that location and Greenwich.

Petrol

You will find petrol difficult to obtain on some sections of the overland route, especially in the desert areas. Information as to where petrol is available is given in the route information sections (pages 137–207); however, in the Reggane/Tessalit section, petrol may not be available for a distance of 800 mls. It is essential that you keep your reserve petrol supplies topped up at all times; you should also bear in mind the high rate of evaporation that will take place because of the extreme heat. As a general rule, your reserve should never fall below 25 per cent. In Zaire, never let your supplies fall below half.

In the costing section (pages 24–27), petrol is estimated at 75p per gallon. However, you must remember that there is a considerable fluctuation in price over the African continent as a whole; in particular, the cost of petrol will increase proportionally to the distance it has to be carried from ports, railheads, etc. It is cheaper in Nigeria, so fill up before going into Cameroun, where it is again cheaper than in the Central African Republic. Petrol coupons are available in Morocco (a maximum of three coupons per day for vehicles over 1,000 cc).

Diesel fuel is cheaper by a third; it can be obtained wherever there is petrol, and also from trucks en route in an emergency.

Photography

Anything which is guarded, or anything which may seem to be of military importance, such as bridges, airports, dams, fire stations, etc., should NOT be photographed. It is also most unwise to be seen photographing any public disorder or disturbance, as mob fury can easily be redirected against the holder of the camera.

Police Controls

Travellers are required to report to all police controls, especially in hazardous areas. Failure to report may incur fines or cause inconvenient hold-ups on a journey. It is not necessary to report in the inhabited areas of the coastal regions of Morocco, Algeria and Tunisia.

Sand Storms

Do not attempt to drive your vehicle in a violent sand storm. It should be parked with the opposite end to the engine facing the wind to prevent silting up. To minimise the dangers of being caught in a sand drift, the vehicle should be driven with deflated tyres, which must be reinflated immediately on reaching harder ground (see also page 63).

Security

This can be classified under two main headings, with regard to the overlander: security of person, and security of possessions.

Personal security is a common-sense matter, which can be achieved by following a few simple rules.

Keep away from lonely places whenever possible, except when in a party.

Do not walk abroad at night down unlit lanes and narrow streets.

Keep away from large crowds proceeding to or leaving sporting events, political meetings, and so on.

Remember: 'discretion before valour'. Never come to grips with an assailant or thief if possible.

Security of possessions will be under constant threat at all times and adequate precautions must be taken to ensure that pilfering is reduced to the minimum. Wherever you are, you will discover an element in society who are always on the look-out for the potential easy target. They will at the slightest opportunity relieve you of your valuables, by stealth or by force. It is therefore essential to maintain a constant surveillance, and to ensure that certain simple precautions are always carried out.

Your vehicle should be fitted with adequate locks and an anti-burglar alarm (see page 51). Make sure these are fully operational whenever the vehicle is left unattended.

Try not to leave your vehicle unattended for long periods, and never at night-time.

Don't spread your equipment about your camp site–only have the essentials to hand.

Don't encourage children by giving them presents or food whilst you are in camp.

Don't give lifts to strangers.

Never, at any time, display your wealth–be it money, jewellery or other valuables. Remember to store all your valuables in a strong-box inside the vehicle at night.

Last, but not least, remember that constant vigilance pays off in the end. Be alert to the situation at all times.

Vehicle disposal

It is illegal to dispose of a vehicle by any means without first paying the import or customs duty which is due.

Vehicle inspections

You should carry out regular inspections of your vehicle and equipment at every stage of your trans-African journey. More specifically, when crossing the Sahara it is in your own interest to make sure that the authorities concerned carry out the necessary inspections before issuing a permit for the next stage of the journey. In spite of regulations (see part 7, Regulations and Information for Crossing the Sahara), some apathy may be shown by the authorities in this respect. It is at all times the motorist's own responsibility to ensure that his vehicle is in a fit condition to negotiate the next stage safely, and that sufficient fuel, water and food is carried.

Warning Triangles

Certain countries require these signs to be placed on the road at the rear of a vehicle (other than a motor-cycle) which is halted on the open road at night; in poor visibility during the day; on a bend of the road; or on a hill.

Water

The population of the British Isles has long been accustomed to regarding the water coming through the mains supply as being completely pure and safe to drink. In very general terms, this still remains true, although increasing pollution and demand make it far from totally safe. Once one travels abroad the dangers are infinitely greater – on the Continent, the inhabitants' caution is emphasised by the inevitable bottle of water on the table.

Of the many ways used by travellers to purify water, the following three are the most common.

Boiling water will make it safe provided it has been boiled long enough. Unfortunately, it takes time to cool, and this leads to a problem of storage and the danger of recontamination. Boiling will not remove dirt, discoloration or rust; it does remove the oxygen from the water, leaving it very 'flat' and distasteful. It is not a practical method when one is on the move in Africa and should really only be employed as a last resort.

Chlorine or other such water-sterilisation tablets can be used. Here, the prime objection is the taste, as one is inclined to drink less when one should be drinking more. It is also necessary to know the level of bacteria in the water, in order to know just how many tablets to add. You should use water-sterilisation tablets for washing all vegetables and fresh fruit, and they are also useful for personal washing facilities.

You are strongly recommended to put all drinking water through a water purification system (see page 53 for details). This is by far the most satisfactory method of removing all chlorine, bacteria and dirt from the water without affecting its natural mineral content. Process only as much water as you need for immediate consumption, and you will find it a very quick and trouble-free procedure.

Water sterilisation is essential on an overland journey across Africa: this cannot be emphasised too strongly. Ignore this rule and you run the risk of contracting a whole range of dysenteries and associated diarrhoeal disorders which, even in their mildest form, can effectively ruin a considerable part of your holiday. It is wise to establish a strict routine at the very start of your journey and then stick to it!

Winter Driving

Certain roads in the Atlas Mountains in Morocco and Algeria will be snowbound in the winter months and you may find it necessary to alter your route to lower altitudes. The inland route via Fez is generally the best to take to Algiers. Normal precautions should be carried out during the winter in these mountainous regions.

Work Permits

It is illegal to work in any of the African countries without a work permit. Overlanders will find it virtually impossible to acquire a work permit—whether temporary or otherwise—in any of the countries they visit; the only possible exceptions to this rule are Rhodesia and the Republic of South Africa.

Part 5
General Information on Countries

Algeria, p. 81 Botswana, p. 82 Cameroun, p. 83 Central African Republic, p. 84 Dahomey, p. 85 Egypt, p. 86 Ghana, p. 87 Ivory Coast, p. 88 Kenya, p. 89 Libya, p. 90 Malawi, p. 90 Mali, p. 91 Mauritania, p. 92 Morocco, p. 93 Mozambique, p. 94 Niger, p. 95 Nigeria, p. 96 Rhodesia, p. 97 Rwanda, p. 98 Senegal, p. 98 South Africa, p. 99 Spanish Sahara, p. 100 Sudan, p. 100 Tanzania, p. 102 Tchad, p. 103 Togo, p. 104 Tunisia, p. 105 Uganda, p. 106 Zaire, p. 106 Zambia, p. 107

Algeria

Formerly a French territory, Algeria became independent on 3rd July 1962 and was declared a Democratic and Popular Republic on 25th September the same year.

The country covers an area of about 900,000 square miles and consists mainly of mountains and desert which offer much in natural beauty. The tourist travelling by car is thus presented with an ever changing panorama of striking gorges, passes and plains where vines, fig, olive and orange trees flourish together with forests of pine, oak and cedar.

Algeria is bounded in the north-west by Morocco and in the east by Tunisia; the Atlas mountains stretch out across, making the boundaries of these two countries. The coastline extends for 750 mls along the Mediterranean Sea where there are to be found beautiful little harbours for the sailing enthusiast, together with charming beaches. It is a country of contrasts, for in the south it is bounded by desert on all sides, extending with great expanses of rolling sand dunes and dried-up wadis, dotted with romantic palm-fringed oases. The Hoggar and Air mountains dominate the

The rocky Atakor region of the Hoggar mountains in Algeria, on the track from Tamanrasset to Ermitage.

desert scene, providing a picturesque backdrop full of pre-historic rock paintings by a race lost in antiquity.

The road system throughout the country is excellent, consisting of trunk and secondary roads in the north and desert tracks in the south, some of which have been recently converted into tarmac roads providing easy access to more distant tourist regions.

Of the three main tracks across the Sahara, the central (Hoggar) route via Tamanrasset is the best. It is the designated route for the proposed Trans-Saharan Highway, part of the great Trans-African Highway of the future. The western route (via Reggane) is difficult and subject to military control. The eastern (Tasssili) route via Djanet is difficult through the mountains and traverses desolate sand seas. It is sketchy into Niger and Tchad and is only possible with four-wheel-drive vehicles with additional supplies of fuel and water, together with an experienced guide.

Algeria can be visited throughout the whole year, although travel in the deep south (Sahara Desert) between May and September is discouraged due to extreme mid-day temperature, which may be in excess of 43 C (110 F). The period from October to the end of May is pleasant. Heavy rain can be expected between November and February, the annual rainfall being concentrated in these months. The four summer months (June to September) are generally warm and humid, the day temperatures registering between 27–32 C (80–90 F), rising when the hot Sirocco blows from the south for brief periods. The best time of the year for a Sahara crossing is at Christmas time, before or after, for this is the coolest time in the desert.

Botswana

Formerly a British Protectorate named Bechuanaland, the country was granted independence on 30th September 1966 and became a Republic with the name of Botswana. It is a member of the British Commonwealth with a population of 650,000.

Botswana occupies an area of 222,000 square miles which is completely landlocked. It is composed of one vast plateau with gently undulating heights of an average altitude of 3,000 ft above sea level. The Kalahari desert covers a great expanse of the centre of the country, with the Okavango river delta flowing into 7,000 square miles of swampland in the north. None of the very few rivers in the country run into the sea, and the southern part of Botswana has very little surface drainage for the little rainfall there is. Because of this and the high temperatures experienced, there is a very high evaporation loss of the little moisture available, which makes the country extremely dry. The main population and towns are located on the eastern edge of the country where the water shortage is not so acute. The major road network therefore tends to run in a north to south direction between Francistown in the north and Gaborone, the capital, in the south. This road also links Botswana to Rhodesia in the north, and the Republic of South Africa in the south.

Climatically the country is sub-tropical with extremes of high and low temperatures. The best time of the year to visit or travel through is in the winter-time in July, when the temperatures are at their lowest.

Cameroun

The Federal Republic of Cameroun was created on 1st October 1961, when the former British Trust Territory of Southern Cameroun elected to join the Republic of Cameroun, which until 1960 was a French Trust Territory.

The Federation became a unitary state on 20th May 1972 under the title of the United Republic of Cameroun, with Yaounde as the capital.

The country covers an area of 183,000 square miles and can be topographically divided into three parts: a region of savanna and steppes from Lake Tchad in the north to the Adamaoua mountain range which runs across the country in a wide north-easterly arc from Mt. Cameroun (13,350 ft) in the south; the equatorial rain forest belt in the coastal region in the south and in the south-west, and between these two a vast scrub-covered and scantily inhabited upland plateau area interlaced with rivers.

Cameroun is bordered in the west by Nigeria, in the north and north-east by Tchad, in the east by the Central African Republic, and in the north by Congo Brazzaville, Gabon, Equatorial Guinea and the sea, of which there is 124 miles of coastline.

The Government has in recent years taken stringent measures

with a view to protecting certain wildlife species liable to become extinct. They have created a number of reserves and parks which are worth a visit; these are the Waza National Park, the Faro Reserve, the Boubandjidah National Park, the Dja Reserve, the Douala-Edea Reserve, the Campo Reserve, the Kalamaloue Reserve, the Bafia Reserve and the Nanga-Eboko Reserve.

A number of hunting encampments have been provided in the majority of the towns in the north. These encampments are known as 'Boucarrou' and are equipped with all modern conveniences.

Climatically the country is full of contrast. In the rain forests to the west and south, it is tropical with high temperatures and humidity, the heaviest rain falling between mid-March and May and from September to November. In the south-east the heavy rains last from June to September or October, with some heavy showers also in April. The coolest part of the year is from July to September and the hottest from December to March. Temperatures range from 19 C to 32 C (67 F to 93 F) in Douala and from 17 C to 29 C (63 F to 88 F) in Yaounde. In the north there is a much drier climate with more extreme temperatures, ranging from 6 C (42 F) at night in January to 43 C (110 F) by day in July. In the mountainous area in the west, the climate varies widely according to altitude and is considerably cooler. Very dusty conditions can be expected in the dry season which may affect the throat and sinuses, and the necessary precautions should be taken.

The road network throughout the country is limited, and surface conditions vary considerably according to climate and terrain. The capital, Yaounde, and the principal towns have bitumenised roads; elsewhere standards are low with surfaces of dirt, gravel or laterite, which is dusty in the dry season and difficult in the wet. The network of feeders is inadequate and extensive upgradings and additional links are scheduled, including the Trans-African Highway project from Lagos, Nigeria to Mombasa, Kenya which will traverse the country.

Central African Republic

Formally a part of the French Equatorial Colonial Administration, known as Oubangui–Chari, it was granted independence in 1958 with the title of Central African Republic.

The country is landlocked covering an area of 238,000 square miles. It is marginally larger than France but has a population of only one and a half million. Topographically it consists of a vast undulating plateau which forms a natural watershed towards Tchad in the north, together with the Oubangui and Congo rivers in the south. The plateau stretches out from the Cameroun border in the north-west to the Bongo Massif near the Sudan border in the north-east, with heights varying between 2–3,000 ft in the west to 4,500 ft in the east. Vegetation ranges from the Sudanese type, such as tamarind in the north-east of the country, to savanna north of the capital Bangui, where in the south-west the equatorial forest begins.

The road network within the country is small. Outside the main towns the roads are mostly dirt and are fair by African standards. In the south-east they are liable to become impassable as a result of extensive inundation during the main rainy season, May to November. Climatically, the best months for visiting or travelling through the country are December to February when the temperatures are as low as 14 C (58 F); at other times of the year they can be as high as 40 C (104 F).

Dahomey

The republic of Dahomey was formerly a French colony and a self-governing member of the French Community. It was granted independence in August 1960.

The country has a population of two and a half million and covers an area of 43,232 square miles. It has a coastline of only 78 mls and extends inland for about 410 mls to the Niger river. Because of its narrow width and greater length the topography of the country varies, as also does the climate. In the south, along the coastal plain, the climate is equatorial with a rainfall of about 50 ins. The plain rises inland to a plateau which is broken in the south by belts of higher ground and in the north-west by the Atakora mountain range which rises to heights of 1,500 ft. Climatically the dry months increase until a tropical climate prevails over the northern half of the country. Here a dry season alternates with a wet one, the latter comprising seven months in the central region and four months in the northern, with a rainfall averaging 50 ins.

All of the principal towns are accessible by road, which are mainly laterite surfaced. There is a first-class tarmac road along the coast, connecting the capital Porto Novo with Cotonou. The roads up country vary according to the seasons: in the south, from March to mid-July and from mid-September to November, temperatures range from 20–34 C (68–93 F) with very high humidity. The northern region experiences one long rainy season between March and October with temperatures as high as 46 C (115 F) between March and April and as low as 10–15 C (50–59 F) in December and January.

Egypt

A republic, Egypt covers an area of 386,200 square miles, some of which–in the Peninsular of Sinai–is Israeli-occupied territory. It has an estimated population of 35½ million.

The country is bounded by the Mediterranean Sea in the north, Israel, Jordan and Saudi Arabia on the east, Sudan on the south and Libya on the west. A greater part of the country in the west and east flanking the river Nile is desert and scrub and is sparsely inhabited. Nearly all the agriculture of the country is centred around the Nile delta which is heavily populated.

The climate is variable. In the winter months of November to March the weather is comparatively cool and dry; average day temperatures are around 18 C (65 F) and the nights are cold. During the spring and summer, day temperatures are between 32 C (90 F) and 38 C (100 F) with spells of intense heat between May and September when the khamsin blows from the desert. Rainfall is negligible throughout the year and the river Nile is harnessed to provide irrigation for cultivation.

All of the main roads along the Mediterranean seaboard, and in the Nile delta and valley are asphalted and are maintained in very good condition, but country roads are dirt-surfaced and become difficult in the wet weather.

The recent Arab–Israeli conflict and ensuing political crisis prohibits foreign tourists motoring within the country, even if they are driving hired cars. Special permits have to be obtained from the Ministry of Interior for each journey. It is therefore advisable to make enquiries before entering the country to ascertain the

The author's wife changes mode of transportation to the ship of the desert at the El Giza Pyramids, Egypt.

regulations in force at the time you may wish to visit.

Ghana

Ghana was created in 1957 from the former British Colonial territories of Gold Coast and British Togoland and at the same time became an independent State within the Commonwealth. In 1964 it was proclaimed a republic.

The country has an estimated population of 8.6 million and borders the Gulf of Guinea. It has a coast line of 350 mls which consists mainly of scrubland and plains interlaced with lagoons near the mouth of the river Volta. On the west it is bounded by Ivory Coast, to the north by Upper Volta and on the east by Togo. Inland lies an extensive forest belt which gives way in the north to open savanna.

The country lies entirely within the tropics, and because of its geographical position the climate is influenced by two main air streams: one, moist and relatively cool from across the Atlantic; the second, continental, hot and dry, a harmattan from across the desert mass of the north-east. These two air streams together produce a hot and humid climate; temperatures tend to rise and humidity to fall as one travels inland from the coast.

The coolest time of the year is approximately between June and September when the main rainfall occurs. There is however very little variation in general temperatures which average between 23 C (73 F) and 30 C (86 F) throughout the year. There are two rainy seasons in the south, one between April and July and the other between September and November, with a total rainfall of 50 to 86 inches. In the north there is one rainy season which occurs between April and September with an average rainfall of 45 to 50 inches.

All the main towns are connected by a system of all-weather roads, many of which are tarred. Secondary roads are of laterite and are liable to be impassable during the rainy season.

Ivory Coast

The Ivory Coast, formerly part of French West Africa, was granted independence in 1960. It has an estimated population of 5.2 million, comprising 60 different tribal groups.

The country covers an area of 127,000 square miles and lies on the Gulf of Guinea. It is bounded in the west by Liberia and the Republic of Guinea, in the north by Mali and Upper Volta, and in the east by Ghana.

There are two distinct geographical zones in the country: one coastal, in the south, consisting of equatorial rain forests; the second in the north, a dry savanna belt stretching across from west to east.

The coastline too, is divided into two topographical features. The coast from the Liberian border to Fresco in the centre is made up of cliffs, rocky promontories and sandy bays. From Fresco to the Ghana border the coast consists of straight sand bars, backed by lagoons.

Climatically the country is tropical, hot and humid in the coastal regions, which have a total rainfall of 50 to 95 inches covering a period of two rainy seasons—the heavier between March and July and the lighter between September and December. In the north there is a single rainy season of five to seven months between April and October, with a rainfall of 50 to 60 inches.

The road network within the country is not large, considering its size; only about one third of the roads are bitumen-surfaced. The remainder are earth roads which vary in condition throughout the country and are severely affected in the rainy season.

Kenya

A former British Colony, Kenya was granted independence in 1963 and became a republic within the Commonwealth in 1964.

The country covers an area of 224,960 square miles and has a population of approximately 11 million. It lies almost exactly astride the equator and has a coastline to the east on the Indian Ocean. To the south and west it is bounded by Tanzania and Uganda, and to the north by Sudan, Ethiopia and the Somali Republic. The coastal plain in the east rises gradually through dry bush to the highlands in the interior which have a base at about 5,000 ft. Here Mt. Kenya dominates the scene at 17,058 ft, together with other heights of 8–10,000 ft. The Kenya Highlands are bisected north and south by the Great Rift Valley. This great natural trough is some 40 miles across in places and is bounded by spectacular escarpments of 2–3,000 ft. Westwards of this region the country descends into the plains of the west and to the shores of Lake Victoria. It is in the Highlands region that the fine arable land is to be found and subsequently the greater population, for much of the country, especially in the north and east, is arid or semi-arid.

Climatically Kenya has a wide range. In the low-lying districts, particularly along the coast, the climate is tropical, hot and humid. In the interior and the highlands the climate is more temperate; here there are normally two periods of rain, the long rains from April to June and the short rains in October and November. Rainfall is heavy, particularly during the long rains, but is generally intermittent. The best time to visit the country is during the drier months.

The road network throughout the country is good and all of the major towns are connected by bitumen-surfaced roads. Feeder roads are earth- or gravel-surfaced and are also kept in good condition, though traffic is liable to interruption or delay in wet weather.

Libya

The Libyan Arab Republic was proclaimed in 1969. It covers an area of 680,000 square miles and has an estimated population of over 2 million.

Libya is bounded by the Mediterranean Sea on the north, Egypt on the east, Sudan on the south-east, Tchad on the south, Algeria on the west and Tunisia on the north-west. The country is a vast plateau intersected by depressions, rising to the south in steps from the low-lying coastal region in the north, with elevations in the south of 12,000 ft in the Tibesti mountains. The country away from the coastal strip consists of large areas of arid scrub and sand seas with scattered oases, the most important of which are Jofra, Sebha, Ghab and Kufra.

The climate along the coastal region is temperate but is influenced by changes in temperature caused by the Sahara mass in the interior. Rainfall is irregular and occurs mostly from October to March. Temperatures are high during summer months but are rarely over 38 C (100 F) except for the deep south where it may be as much as 48 C (120 F).

The road network in the country is concentrated along the coastal strip, where an asphalt National Highway runs for 1,140 miles from the Tunisian border to Egypt: spur roads run southwards for short distances to centres of habitation but are few in number.

As special regulations for foreigners entering the Republic are at present in force, visitors to the country are advised to make enquiries as to the regulations that are in force at the time of visiting.

Malawi

Formerly known as Nyasaland, a part of the British Colonial territory of the Federation of Rhodesia and Nyasaland, Malawi became independent in 1964, becoming a republic within the Commonwealth in 1966.

The republic covers an area of 45,747 square miles, which includes

Lake Malawi, and has an estimated population of 4.5 million, of which the greater part resides in the central and southern regions.

Malawi is a long narrow, landlocked country of scenic beauty, bounded on the east for three-quarters of its length by Lake Malawi and surrounded by Tanzania, Mozambique and Zambia. It is situated in the continuation of the East African Rift Valley and is basically a plateau country of varying heights: from Lake Malawi at 1,550 ft above sea level, to elevations in the north of 5,000 ft to 8,000 ft, in the centre of 2,500 ft to 4,500 ft and in the southern region of 6,000 ft to 10,000 ft.

Climatically the country is tropical and generally has a high rainfall which mainly falls between December and March. The summer season runs from September to April and the hottest months are October to November, prior to the rainy season. There is little rain between April and August, which makes it an ideal time for a visit as it is also the coolest time of the year. Because of the varying altitudes, temperatures range from 15 C (59 F) to 26 C (79 F).

The central and southern regions are linked by good asphalt or well-maintained gravel roads. The roads in the northern region are not so good and are unsurfaced. Minor roads and tracks vary considerably depending on the location and time of the year; some journeys can be quite arduous.

Mali

Formerly known as the French Saudan, a part of French West Africa, Mali became a republic in 1960 emerging out of a federation with Senegal. The country is landlocked and covers an area of 465,000 square miles having an approximate population of about 5 million.

Topographically Mali is situated in the centre of west Africa and is bounded by Senegal in the west, Mauritania and Algeria in the north, Niger to the east, Upper Volta and Ivory Coast to the south, and Guinea to the south-west. Almost one half of the country is desert or semi-desert and consequently very dry. The rainy season begins in June and continues until the end of October; almost the entire annual rainfall of 40–50 ins occurs in this period. With the advent of the rains, the temperature drops but humidity rises rapidly to an average of about 80 per cent in August and September. The coolest months and the best time to visit the country is between late November and early February. After February the weather gets progressively hotter and drier with shade temperatures ranging between 46 C and 49 C (115 F and 120 F).

The road network in the country is small, and only about 4,350 miles out of a total of 6,500 miles of the road system are usable throughout the year. Asphalted roads total about 1,000 mls. Travelling by road within the country is therefore difficult.

Mauritania

A former French West African territory, it became an independent republic in 1960. The country stretches from the Senegal river in the south, to the Sahara Desert and Algeria in the north, bordered by the Atlantic and Spanish Sahara in the west and Mali in the east. It covers an area of about 420,000 square miles, having an estimated population of one and a half million, of whom 75 per cent are nomads.

Geographically the country is a part of the great Saharan region and is consequently very arid. The region in the south bordering the Senegal river supports most of the population, for it is here that the seasonal flooding of the river provides enough moisture to the earth to allow cultivation to take place.

Climatically the country is hot with temperatures between 18 C and 29 C (65 F and 85 F) during the dry season from December to May. In the south frequent thunderstorms occur from June to November, with rain up to 24 ins in the year. In the north during this time rainfall is absent or negligible and temperatures may be very high.

The road network in the country is extremely small, consisting mostly of local tracks, except between Rosso, Nouakchott and Atar which has now been asphalted throughout.

It is not advisable to visit the country during the months of June and December due to the extreme heat and shortage of water in the northern regions.

One of the many spectacular scenes of the Atlas Mountains—the Todra Gorge, Morocco.

Morocco

Formerly a Spanish and French Protectorate, Morocco was granted independence in 1956. The country, a monarchy, covers an area of approximately 180,000 mls and has an estimated population of $15\frac{1}{2}$ million.

Geographically, Morocco is situated in the north-west corner of Africa and has coastlines on the Atlantic and the Mediterranean.

It is further bounded by Algeria in the east, Mauritania in the south and Spanish Sahara in the south-west. A dominant feature in the country are the Atlas mountains, which rise out of the south-west and continue to the Algerian border in the north-east with elevations of up to 13,000 ft in the south-west. On the Atlantic side of these mountains there is an extensive fertile plain which supports the majority of the inhabitants. The southern aspects of the mountain ranges descend and merge in a series of steppes into the Sahara Desert.

Morocco enjoys a moderate climate in the winter with an average temperature of 15 C (60 F) between November and May. During the summer months, June to September, temperatures of 38 C (100 F) and over may be expected.

There is an excellent network of roads throughout the country. Surfaces are very good along the Atlantic and Mediterranean coast and directly inland to the main towns of Meknes, Fes, Oujda, Erfoud, Kasba Tadla, Marrakech, Ouarzazate and Taroudannt. Country roads and lateral spurs range from surfaced roads to gravel and dirt tracks, the latter in the desert regions.

Mozambique

Formerly a Portuguese African territory, Mozambique became an independent republic in June 1975. It covers an area of 302,328 sq mls and has an estimated population of 8 million of whom about 180,000 are Europeans.

Mozambique lies on the east coast of Africa and is bounded in the north by Tanzania, on the west by Malawi, Zambia and Rhodesia, and in the south-west by the Republic of South Africa. The country lies south of the Equator and is for a greater part in the tropics. It can be basically divided into three zones; coastal lowlands, middle plateau and northern plateau bordering on to Malawi and Tanzania; the plateaux vary in height between 800 ft to 2,000 ft.

Climatically the country is divided into two main seasons, a hot wet season from October to March and a cooler dry season from April to September. Temperatures can vary between 23 C (73 F) and 43 C (110 F). Most of the rainfall occurs during the second half of the hot season, during which time the humidity is also the greatest. The best time to visit the country is between May and July.

Because of the greater emphasis on communications by rail, the road network was sadly neglected. The recent internal problems that have beset the country have started a programme of road improvements which is connecting Rhodesia and South Africa with asphalt roads from the port of Beira. Roads in the northern part of the country are still very difficult to traverse especially in the rainy season, and movement north and south from the Tanzanian border is hampered by the numerous rivers that have to be crossed.

Travellers intending to enter Mozambique are advised to make careful enquiries as to the political feelings of the new national government of the republic, as some curtailment of travel may be imposed.

Niger

The republic emerged out of one of the territories that was once part of French West Africa. It was granted independence in August 1960. Niger is bounded in the north by Algeria and Libya, in the east by Tchad, in the south by Nigeria, Dahomey and Upper Volta and in the west by Mali. It is completely landlocked and covers an area of 459,000 sq mls, having an estimated population of 4 million.

Niger is the largest landlocked country in west Africa. It is a vast plateau approximately 1,200 ft above sea level, split by the Niger river in the south-west, whose seasonally flooded valley provides the major proportion of the country's cultivation and pasture for livestock. Two-thirds of the country is desert and uninhabited. In the north on the Libyan border there are massifs with heights of about 2,600 ft and in the centre of the country the Air mountains rise to a height of 6,000 ft. Apart from the savanna type strip, broadly 100 mls wide running along the Nigerian border, the whole of the country north is a vast desert.

Climatically, a hot desert climate prevails throughout except in the south-west which is subject to tornadoes during August. There are basically two seasons, one dry from October to May, the other humid from June to October when the annual rainfall of 9 to 30 ins occurs. The heaviest rain falls in August. The harmattan, a cool wind which blows across the desert, provides inspite of its dusty atmosphere cool and refreshing early mornings and evenings.

Because of the nature of the country the road network is extremely small and only about 250 mls are asphalted or sealed. These are mainly in the vicinity of the Nigerian border. Other roads are merely desert tracks which are difficult to negotiate. The best time for a visit is between October and May.

Nigeria

A former British Colonial territory, Nigeria was granted independence in October 1960 and is now a Federal Republic within the Commonwealth.

The country covers an area of 356,669 sq mls and has an estimated population of 69 million, the greatest in Africa.

Nigeria is bounded on the west by Dahomey, in the north by Niger and Tchad, and in the east by Cameroun; in the south it has a coastline of about 500 mls on the Gulf of Guinea.

Topography and vegetation vary considerably throughout the

A typical native market in Nigeria—not the place to buy your meat . . .

country; in the south it is hot and humid, the climate being influenced by the warm damp air stream from the sea. In this area swamp and tropical rain forests abound. Inland the country becomes more open and merges into savanna and open woodland, rising to a central plateau at about 6,000 ft. The extreme northern part of the country borders onto the encroaching desert and is hot and dry.

The wet and dry seasons are well defined. In the north the rainy season extends from April to September and day-time temperatures may reach 43 C (110 F) and can drop to below 4 C (40 F) at night. During the winter in the dry season the harmattan wind blows across from the Sahara Desert, carrying very fine dust which causes a haze; the mornings and evenings are generally delightfully cool. The rainy season in the south extends from March to November and the average temperature is about 29 C (85 F) with a high humidity which increases during the rainy season.

The road network throughout the country is excellent and all the major towns are connected by sealed roads. Some difficulty can however be experienced in the country areas during the rains, and travellers are advised that the best time of the year to visit is between October and March.

Rhodesia

A self-governing British territory whose government unilaterally declared its independence of the British Crown in 1965, Rhodesia continues, inspite of the present political dilemma, to be part of Her Majesty's dominions.

The country covers an area of 150,300 sq mls and is completely landlocked. It is bounded in the north by Tanzania, to the east by Malawi and Mozambique, in the south by South Africa, in the south-west by Botswana, and in the west by Zambia. It has an estimated population of 5½ million, of which over 300,000 are of European stock.

Rhodesia consists of a number of plateau regions of between 3,000 ft and 8,503 ft above sea level. Because of this it has a moderate climate with temperatures varying between regions, depending on elevation. The main rainy season is between November and March, except on the eastern highlands where it is variable.

All of the major roads are asphalted between the larger towns. Country and minor roads are murram-surfaced or dirt, and may only be difficult in the wet weather.

Rwanda

A former United Nations Trust territory known as Ruanda-Urundi, administered by Belgium, Rwanda became an independent republic in 1962.

The country is small—only 10,166 sq mls, landlocked, mountainous and has an estimated population of 4 million. It is bounded by Uganda in the north, Tanzania in the east, Burundi in the south and Zaire in the west, and lies at an altitude of between 4,790 ft and 15,000 ft above sea level.

The countryside is intensively cultivated and is intersected by deep, narrow, fertile valleys and a number of small lakes. There is a well developed road system throughout the country. Roads wind through gorges with tumbling waterfalls and up over picturesque escarpments with breathtaking views. The surfaces are dusty, bumpy and composed of a mixture of dirt, gravel and laterite. They are poorly maintained and travel over them is slow. Camp sites are difficult to find due to the nature of the country, and the police should always be asked to advise as to the whereabouts of a suitable site.

The climate of Rwanda is tropical, but because of its altitude temperatures range between 23 C (73 F) and 13 C (55 F). There are two rainy seasons in the year, the main one being from mid-January to mid-May and the other from mid-October to mid-December. Rainfall is heavy and makes driving on the mountain roads very difficult. The best time therefore to visit the country is between the rains, or between June and September.

Senegal

A former French West African territory, Senegal became an independent republic in 1960. The country is bounded in the west by the

Atlantic seaboard, in the north by Spanish Sahara and Mauritania, in the east by Mali, and in the south by the Republic of Guinea and Portuguese Guinea. Gambia is an enclave in the country to the south.

Senegal covers an area of 76,000 sq mls and has an estimated population of nearly 4 million, of whom some 67,000 are non-African. The country is predominantly flat, dry and featureless, being not much more than 300 ft above sea level except for some high eastern and south-eastern borderlands.

Climatically the Atlantic seaboard areas are breezy and cool, having a rainy season of about four months, average temperatures being between 18 C and 31 C (66 F and 88 F). Inland both temperatures and rainfall are higher with a longer rainy season, June to November, which in turn increases humidity. Natural vegetation throughout most of the country is of the savanna type together with large areas of arid semi-desert.

All the large towns are connected by all-weather roads which are good within the towns' environs but deteriorate as one travels inland, especially towards the Mali frontier. This is best reached by rail from Dakar, for the roads are generally impossible during the rainy season.

The best time of the year to visit Senegal is between December and May, when it is cooler and when the roads are not affected by the rains.

South Africa

The Republic of South Africa was established in 1961 when the former Union of South Africa withdrew from the Commonwealth. The Republic covers an area of over 472,000 sq mls and has an estimated population of 21.5 million, of whom nearly 4 million are European.

South Africa has a coastline on both the South Atlantic and Indian Oceans. It is bordered by South West Africa in the north-west, Botswana in the north and Rhodesia, Mozambique and Swaziland in the north-east. The country consists mainly of a high plateau ranging up to 7,000 ft above sea level, fringed by steep mountain ranges and a narrow coastal strip below 1,500 ft. Because of the few rivers in the interior, water supplies are scarce and the north central regions are desert or dry veld.

The climate of South Africa is for the most part sub-tropical with some regional variations. Altitude, too, has a decided influence on temperatures and rainfall. The summer months from November to February are generally warm and dry. Rain falls mainly in the winter, from May to September, but does not disrupt movement on the main roads. The low-lying central regions are hot in summer-time and humidity may rise in some areas.

The country has an excellent system of national roads in which all the large towns are linked by asphalt-surfaced roads. Minor roads also, in country areas, are maintained in very good condition.

Spanish Sahara

A desert territory of approximately 102,702 sq mls, governed as a Province of Spain, Spanish Sahara has a population of approximately 72,000, including 25,000 Europeans of whom about 15,000 are soldiers. It is bounded on the west by the Atlantic, to the north by Morocco, to the east by Algeria and to the east and south by Mauritania.

The territory is a flat desert waste, mostly of sand and rock rising inland from the coast, with intermittent zones of cultivation where there is water. The country is extremely arid due to the erratic rainfall which in some years is negligible.

Temperatures vary greatly and can range from 10 C (50 F) to over 48 C (120 F) in the summer. Travel through the country should therefore only be undertaken in the winter when the day temperatures are at their lowest.

The general network of roads and tracks is extremely small and journeys between places of habitation can be very hazardous for the inexperienced desert traveller. A four-wheeled vehicle is vital if journeys are to be made into the interior.

Sudan

The Democratic Republic of the Sudan became an independent

state in 1956. It lies wholly within the Tropics and is almost entirely landlocked except for a part of its eastern border with the Red Sea. It is bounded by Libya and Egypt in the north, Tchad, Central African Republic and Zaire in the west, Uganda and Kenya in the south and Ethiopia in the south-east.

The country's most prominent physical features are the rivers, the White and Blue Niles. Their headwaters rise in Uganda and Ethiopia respectively, joining at Khartoum to form the main river Nile, which flows northwards to Egypt and the Mediterranean. The river splits the country into two and provides the main agricultural belt and means of communication riverwise.

Climatically the country may be divided into four regions. North of latitude 19N is a desert region where dry northerly winds prevail throughout the year and rain is rare. Between latitude 19N and latitude 10N is a semi-arid region which has very little binding vegetation and is subject to duststorms. The little rain that does fall is in the mid-summer. South of latitude 10N the country has a variety of vegetation, scrub, forests and vast areas of swamp land. The climate is humid with rainfall spread fairly evenly over the year, though it is slightly drier in the winter months. The coastal region bordering the Red Sea is profoundly influenced by the sea. Most of the rain falls in the winter, though there is a subsidiary rainy season in the summer corresponding to the rainy season inland.

Average maximum temperatures at Khartoum range from 31 C (89 F) in January to 41 C (107 F) in May and June.

The best season for visiting most parts of the Sudan is between October and mid-April. From mid-April until the end of June the weather becomes extremely hot and dry. Through from July to September the temperature drops with the onset of the rains, and the climate becomes more humid. At this period road travel outside the towns becomes difficult, if not impossible. December, January and February are relatively pleasant.

The southern provinces, which are somewhat cooler and more humid, may be visited during the summer months.

Most rural roads are rough tracks, many having numerous stretches of soft sand, and these conditions demand a very robust type of vehicle with exceptionally high clearance. In the northern part of the country most of the roads are closed during the rainy season from July to September. Soil conditions are more favourable in the south and a number of roads there, though unsurfaced, are passable throughout the year.

Travellers intending to make car journeys through the country should make certain that the roads are open, and that permission to travel on them is likely to be granted, before setting out on their journey.

Tanzania

Formerly known as Tanganyika and a British Mandate territory, Tanzania was granted independence in 1961. In 1964 Zanzibar united with Tanzania and the two countries became the United Republic of Tanzania, a member of the Commonwealth.

The two countries cover a total area of 343,038 sq mls, of which there is 20,650 sq mls of inland water in Tanzania. The estimated population is about 13 million, 360,000 of whom live in the islands of Zanzibar and Pemba off the Tanzanian coast in the Indian Ocean.

Tanzania is bounded by Kenya, Lake Victoria and Uganda in the north, by Rwanda, Burundi and Lake Tanganyika in the west, Zambia, Malawi and Lake Malawi in the south-west, Mozambique in the south and the Indian Ocean with 500 mls of coastline in

Hippos sport in the Orangi river in the Serengeti National Park, Tanzania.

the east. It has some of the highest and lowest parts in Africa – Mt Kilimanjaro at 19,520 ft, and the floor of Lake Tanganyika, at 1,175 ft below sea level. The country away from the coast is made up of a number of undulating plateaux and depressed areas. In the north and central areas the greatest heights are to be found.

The climate throughout the country varies from place to place. The coastal region is generally hot and humid for most of the year; inland the temperatures fall, as also the humidity. Temperatures may exceed 32 C (90 F) and may be as low as 15 C and 21 C (60 F and 70 F) in the inhabited areas, depending on altitude. The rainy season for a greater part of the country is between December and May; heavy rain may be expected to fall in the two periods October to November, and April to May, in some areas.

The network of roads is small for the size of the country and conditions vary. The road from Dar es Salaam to the Kenyan border for Nairobi and to Tunduma on the Zambian border is asphalted; other roads are murram- or dirt-surfaced and many become impassable in the rainy seasons.

Tchad

Formerly part of French Equatorial Africa, the Republic of Tchad was granted independence in August 1960.

It has a population of $3\frac{1}{2}$ million and covers an area of 501,000 sq mls. It is the largest of the landlocked countries in Africa and comprises three distinct regions. The northern region, arising out of the Lake Tchad depression, is one of sparse scrub vegetation, gradually attaining altitude as it stretches out to the north to the mountainous Sahara region of the Tibesti where heights of 11,000 ft are recorded. The central region is a natural watershed with the Chari and Logone rivers flowing north to feed Lake Tchad; this is an area of open grassland with a rainfall of 10 to 20 ins a year. The southern region has a rainfall in excess of 20 ins and may be as extreme as 47 ins. It is an area of savanna and woodland vegetation and can be extremely difficult to travel through in the rainy season.

In the past, Tchad was traditionally a focal point for Saharan and equatorial African trade routes, which have today taken other

The author crossing the confluence of the Logone and Chari rivers in Tchad, by means of a dugout canoe.

paths, thus affecting the modernisation of the country's road network. Roads are fair by African standards and are mostly dirt outside the main towns; many of them are only motorable in the dry season.

Climatically the best months are December and January, but visits or transit through Tchad can be undertaken between November and May.

Togo

A former German colony, Togo was divided into two League of Nations Mandates in 1918. The western part was allocated to Great Britain and became an integral part of Ghana in 1956 following a United Nations sponsored plebiscite. The larger western area was allocated to France and also became an autonomous republic within the French Union in 1956. It later achieved independence as the

Republic of Togo in 1960.

Togo covers an area of 21,000 sq mls and has an estimated population of 2 million. It is the smallest of the African states formerly associated with France and is bounded on the west by Ghana, in the north by Upper Volta and in the east by Dahomey. It has a coastline of 35 mls on the Gulf of Guinea and extends inland for about 400 mls. The maximum width of the country is no more than 100 mls.

The climate is pleasant, as it is never excessively hot. The average temperatures on the coast are about 27 C (80 F) and inland about 30 C (86 F). The humidity, however, rises during the rainy seasons, of which there are two: the greater from April to July and the lesser from October to November. The dry period is from January to March and it is comparatively cool from December to January when the harmattan winds blow down from the north. This is the best time for a visit.

The road network throughout the republic is good, but away from the coast the roads are mostly of laterite construction, which may cause a little difficulty in some areas in the wet weather.

Tunisia

A former French protectorate, Tunisia was granted independence in 1956. It has an area of 63,362 sq mls and an estimated population of 5½ million.

The republic is bounded on the north and east by a 750-ml coastline on the Mediterranean sea, on the south-east by Libya, and on the south and west by Algeria. The northern part of the country is mountainous, being an extension of the Atlas mountains which form the backdrop for the narrow coastal plain and the desert in the interior to the south.

Tunisia has a true Mediterranean climate: hot dry summers followed by warm wet winters. Temperatures from May to mid-October vary between 30 C (85 F) and 37 C (100 F) with little rainfall except during late September and in October. Rain is frequent during the winter months from December to the end of March, with average temperatures during the day of 13 C (55 F) and cooler evenings and nights.

The country has an excellent network of asphalt or macadam

roads between all the major towns and to all the important tourist centres of interest. Interior roads vary and are generally only dirt- or gravel-surfaced and poor sections will be encountered.

Uganda

A former British Protectorate, Uganda was granted independence in 1962 and became a republic within the Commonwealth in 1963.

The country has an estimated population of about 9½ million and covers an area of 93,981 sq mls, of which 18 per cent is made up of freshwater lakes and swamps.

Uganda is entirely landlocked and is bounded in the north by Sudan, in the east by Kenya, in the south by Tanzania and Rwanda, and in the west by Zaire.

It is largely a plateau country with heights varying between 3,000 ft and 5,000 ft above sea level, and because of this it has a modified equatorial climate with little seasonal variations.

There are normally two periods of rain, the long rains from April to June and the short rains in October and November. Rainfall is heavy during the long rains, but is not continuous. The coolest time of the year is between July and September and this is the best time for a visit.

The road network within the republic is good by tropical African standards. There are tarmac and asphalt roads radiating out from the capital Kampala, to the Zaire frontier in the west, towards Gulu in the north and to Nairobi, Kenya in the east. The environs of Kampala are serviced by excellent sealed roads. Country roads are mostly of all-weather murram between the smaller towns and the lesser bush roads are of dirt. These latter roads are difficult to negotiate in the wet weather.

Zaire

Formerly a Belgian colonial territory, the Zaire Republic emerged out of the Democratic Republic of the Congo (Kinshasa) which was granted independence in 1960. Zaire is one of the largest countries in Africa, with an area of 900,000 sq mls, and has an estimated population of nearly 22 million.

It lies astride the equator in the very heart of Africa, bounded in the west by the People's Republic of the Congo, known as Congo (Brazzaville), in the north by the Central African Republic and Sudan, in the east by Uganda, Rwanda, Burundi and Tanzania, in the south by Zambia and Angola. It has also in the west a 25-mile-long seaboard with the Atlantic on the estuary of the Zaire (Congo) river.

Geographically the country comprises widely different features, from great equatorial rain forests in the centre, to dryer savanna bordering the Sudan in the north and Angola in the south. There is also a mountainous area in the south-east with elevations of 8,070 ft above sea level.

The central region has an equatorial climate with rainfall plentiful in all seasons and an average temperature of 26 C (79 F). In the mountainous areas the temperatures are around 18 C (64 F). In the south, south-west and east the main rainy seasons are from October to April/May. In the north there are two seasons, April to June and September to October.

Because of the vast river network throughout the country and the thick equatorial forests, the road network is poor for a country of its size. Only the main centres of habitation and trade are linked up by river transportation. Roads are generally rough and unreliable outside the inhabited areas and receive inadequate maintenance.

Zambia

Formerly the British Protectorate of Northern Rhodesia, Zambia became an independent republic within the Commonwealth in 1964. It covers an area of 290,586 sq mls and has a population of about 4¼ million.

The country is completely landlocked, bordered in the north-west by Zaire, in the north-east by Tanzania, in the east by Malawi, in the south-east by Mozambique, in the south by Rhodesia and the Caprive Strip (an extension of South West Africa), and in the west by Angola. It is mainly a plateau country with elevations of between 3,500 ft and 4,500 ft above sea level, covered with stunted woodland of mixed deciduous and evergreen trees. Three-quarters of the country acts as a watershed for the Zambesi river.

The climate of Zambia, due to its high elevation, is seldom unpleasantly hot. There are three main seasons: from May to August it is cool and dry, from September to November it is hot and dry, and from December to April it is warm and wet. Temperatures vary between 10 C (50 F) and 31 C (88 F) depending on altitude and the time of the year.

There is a good network of roads throughout the country, and all the major towns are connected by tarmac or asphalt-surfaced roads. Minor roads are of gravel and earth and should only be tackled with a robust vehicle.

The best time to visit the country is between May and August.

Part 6
Currency Regulations

The following data has been based on information taken from *Hints to Businessmen*, by permission of the controller of HMSO. It should be used as a guide only. You should always make your own enquiries on the current regulations in force at the time you are travelling, as they are subject to change at short notice. In all cases, you should consult your bank for current rates of exchange.

Algeria

With the exception of gold coins, any amount of foreign currency may be taken into the country. Algerian bank notes are, however, restricted to DA50 per visitor.

Travellers who intend taking currency out of the country must obtain a certificate from the customs officer at the port of entry showing the amount of currency taken into Algeria. This document must be produced and duly endorsed, whenever foreign currency is exchanged for Algerian currency for use in Algeria, and must be shown to the customs on departure. Failure to comply with these regulations will render the traveller liable to forfeit the currency.

Visitors should avoid changing more foreign currency into dinars than they are likely to require as it is extremely difficult to reconvert Algerian dinars. Changing money can often be difficult in Algeria. There are Bureaux de Change at the airports but they will not always accept travellers' cheques; they will sometimes only change foreign bank notes. The only institution officially authorised to change traveller's cheques in Algiers is the Banque Nationale d'Algerie. The Hotel Aletti in Algiers will accept traveller's cheques in payment for bills; there are also facilities available from time to time at the Hotel St. George and at the town office of Air Algerie.

The official unit of currency is the Algerian dinar (DA) divided into 100 centimes. The denominations in circulation are:

Notes: 5, 10, 50 and 100 dinars
Coins: 1 dinar; 1, 5, 20 and 50 centimes

Botswana

There is no restriction on the amount of Botswana currency to be taken into or out of the country.

The unit of currency is the South African rand (R). For the notes and coinage in circulation see under South Africa.

Cameroun

Visitors are allowed to take an unlimited amount of currency into Cameroun but the total amount should be declared; up to 25,000 CFA francs may be taken out if visitors are going to a non-franc country, plus any unspent foreign currency.

The currency in use in the republic is the CFA (Communauté Financière Africaine) franc. The denominations in circulation are:

> Notes: 100, 500, 1,000 and 5,000 CFA francs
> Coins: 1, 2, 5, 10, 25, 50 and 100 CFA francs

Central African Republic

There is no limit to the amount of foreign currency which may be taken into the Central African Republic or Tchad but the export of foreign currency is rigidly controlled.

Sterling traveller's cheques can be cashed, although sometimes French franc cheques are more easily converted. It is as well to limit encashments to requirements, as only 10,000 CFA francs can be taken out of each country and CFA francs are not easily exchanged in non-franc zone territories.

The unit of currency is the CFA (Communauté Financière Africaine) franc which is divided into 100 centimes.

Dahomey

There are no restrictions on the amount of local or foreign currencies which may be taken into Dahomey or Togo, but this should be declared on entry. The amount taken out must not exceed that taken into the countries.

The unit of currency in Dahomey and Togo is the CFA (Communauté Financière Africaine) franc.

The following denominations are in circulation:

Notes: 50, 100, 500, 1,000 and 5,000 CFA francs
Coins: 1, 2, 5, 10, 25 and 100 CFA francs

Egypt

Visitors are not allowed to take Egyptian currency into or out of the country. Any amount of foreign currency, drafts and traveller's cheques may be taken into Egypt, but the amount taken out must not exceed the amount taken in. Visitors are required to complete a currency declaration form on entering and they are advised in their own interests to observe this formality carefully. Under present arrangements a copy of the currency declaration must be retained for presentation to the customs authorities on leaving Egypt.

Traveller's cheques and currency can only be exchanged with authorised foreign exchange dealers, but certain hotels may accept them for payment of bills.

Tourists are requested to transfer a minimum of £30 sterling as a condition of entry.

The unit of currency is the Egyptian pound (£E) divided into 100 piastres (PT) and 1,000 milliemes (mms).

The denominations in circulation are:

Notes:
National and Central Bank of Egypt: 1, 5 and 10
Egyptian pounds; 25 and 50 piastres
Government Treasury; 5 and 10 piastres

113

Coins:
Nickel: 1, 5 and 10 piastres
Copper: $\frac{1}{2}$, 1 and 2 piastres
Brass: $\frac{1}{2}$, 1 and 2 piastres
Aluminium: $\frac{1}{2}$ and 1 piastre

Care should be taken not to confuse the aluminium $\frac{1}{2}$ and 1 PT coins with the nickel 5 and 10 PT coins. (The latter have a milled edge.)

Ghana

Apart from the special case mentioned below, visitors are not permitted to take Ghanaian currency into the country, but there is no restriction on the amount of foreign currency and traveller's cheques that can be taken in. Travellers returning to Ghana may import Ghanaian currency notes which they have previously been permitted to take out of the country (up to a limit of c20), the details of which were duly recorded in their passport at the time of departure.

Under the Exchange Control Act, 1961, travellers are obliged to declare the full amount of foreign and local currency in their possession when entering Ghana. (As far as local currency is concerned the Act is, of course, intended to apply to those travellers returning with local currency, details of which have been previously recorded as described above.) Such a declaration must be made on Exchange Control Form T5. Forms T5 are normally distributed to the traveller at the port or place of entry. The duly completed form should be submitted for certification at the point of entry. The original copy will be returned to the traveller and the duplicate retained by the Exchange Control Authority. Visitors should retain their copy of the Form T5 as this must be surrendered to the authorities at the port or place of departure from Ghana.

Travellers may exchange their foreign currency into local currency only with authorised dealers, namely, any bank in Ghana. Details of each transaction must be entered on the Form T5.

Visitors are permitted to take out of the country any unused, imported foreign exchange provided that its importation was declared on Form T5 upon entry. On departure any unused local currency must be reconverted into foreign currency, the details of which must be entered on Form T5.

The unit of currency is the cedi (c) divided into 100 pesewas (P). The rate of exchange is subject to slight fluctuation, roughly in line with the movement of the dollar against £ sterling.

The following denominations are in circulation:

Notes: 1, 5 and 10 cedis
Coins: ½, 1, 2½, 5, 10 and 20 pesewas

Ivory Coast

There is no limit to the amount of local or foreign currency which can be taken into each of the countries, but all exports of foreign currency, except to Metropolitan France, are rigidly controlled by the Office des Changes. The usual amount visitors are allowed to take out is 125,000 CFA francs.

Traveller's cheques and other banking instruments, if correctly endorsed, are accepted in accordance with normal practice, and foreign currency which would normally be accepted by European exchanges can be exchanged.

The unit of currency in the Ivory Coast and Niger is the CFA (Communauté Financière Africaine) franc, which is also legal tender in Dahomey, Senegal and Togo. The CFA franc is circulated in the following denominations:

Notes: 100, 500, 1,000 and 5,000 CFA francs (The 100-franc note is being replaced by a 100-franc coin)
Coins: 1, 5, 10, 25 and 100 CFA francs

Kenya

Visitors are not allowed to take into or out of the country any Kenyan currency. Other currency should be declared to the customs authorities on arrival. There is no limit to the amount of traveller's cheques, letters of credit, etc.

Kenyan currency is not redeemable outside East Africa.

The unit of currency is the Kenya shilling (Sh.), divided into 100 cents. 20 shillings = 1 Kenya £. The following denominations are in circulation:

> Notes: 5, 10, 20, 50 and 100 shillings
> Coins: 1 shilling, 2 shillings; 5, 10, 25 and 50 cents

Libya

A visitor is not permitted to have more than 20 Libyan dinars in bank notes in his possession on entering or leaving the country. There is no restrictions on the amount of other currencies, credit notes or traveller's cheques. All currencies, traveller's cheques, etc., must be declared on entry and departure and the amount taken out of the country must not exceed that taken in. Forms are issued at frontier posts on which this declaration must be made. Care must be taken not to lose the form which will be required on departure.

The unit of currency is the Libyan dinar (LD) divided into 1,000 dirhams. The dinar succeeded the Libyan pound which ceased to be the unit of currency on 31st August 1971.

The following denominations are in circulation:

> Notes: $\frac{1}{4}$, $\frac{1}{2}$, 1, 5 and 10 Libyan dinars
> (Notes for $\frac{1}{4}$, $\frac{1}{2}$, 1, 5 and 10 Libyan pounds continue to circulate and are used alongside the new currency)
> Coins: 1, 5, 10, 20, 50 and 100 milliemes (dirhams)
> (New coins have not yet been issued)

The name piastre, which was formerly an official unit of currency when the Libyan pound was divided into 100 piastres, is now used colloquially to denote units of 10 dirhams.

Malawi

Malawi currency up to a maximum of K20 in value may be taken in and a similar sum may be taken out. However, it should be noted that Malawi currency cannot be repatriated through the banking system; consequently, visitors are advised to use traveller's cheques and ensure that they do not leave the country with any local currency. Foreign currency may be imported without restriction but only the equivalent of K20 may be taken out. Visitors who take in foreign currency in excess of the equivalent of K20 should declare the currency to a customs officer who will issue a certificate to enable the visitor to export an amount in excess of the normal allowance.

The unit of currency is the Kwacha (K) which is divided into 100 tambala (t.).

Mali

Visitors may bring an unlimited amount of foreign currency into the country and, provided that they declare it on arrival, may take out up to the same quantity. Malian currency may not be taken out of the country.

Traveller's cheques and certain foreign currencies can be exchanged at the Banque de la Republique du Mali and at its branches and the other banks in Bamako.

The local currency is the Malian franc.

Mauritania

An express authority from the Office des Changes of the Banque Centrale des Etats de l'Afrique de l'Ouest is required before foreign currency may be exported from Senegal. Visitors from abroad are, however, permitted to take into or out of Senegal any amount of foreign currency provided that it is declared on entry and departure and that the amount taken out does not exceed the amount taken in.

Not more than 25,000 CFA francs may be taken into or out of Senegal and Mauritania.

Traveller's cheques can be cashed at banks and at certain hotels.

Visitors should ensure that their cheques are made negotiable in Senegal and/or Mauritania.

The currency of Senegal and Mauritania is the CFA (Communauté Financière Africaine) franc. The denominations in circulation are:

Notes: 500, 1,000 and 5,000 CFA francs
Coins: 1, 2, 5, 10, 25, 50 and 100 CFA francs

Morocco

No Moroccan currency whatever may be imported or exported by travellers.

Foreign currency may be imported freely; the amount exported by a visitor may not exceed the amount brought in, but a written declaration on arrival is no longer required.

Moroccan currency purchased by a visitor during his stay may, subject to certain limitations, be re-exchanged for foreign currency on production of bank vouchers relating to the purchase.

The unit of currency is the dirham (DH) which is divided into 100 centimes.

The following denominations are in circulation:

Notes: 5, 10, 50 and 100 dirhams
Coins: 1, and 5 dirhams; 1, 2, 5, 10, 20 and 50 centimes

Mozambique

Travellers entering and leaving Mozambique are required to declare their currency holdings. The amount which may be taken out is limited to a sum not exceeding that taken in, and may include up to Esc 2,500 in local currency. Travellers to Portuguese territories may take out Esc 2,500 in Portuguese currency for tourist and travel expenses.

Traveller's cheques endorsed 'Valid in all countries' are acceptable.

The unit of currency is the Mozambique escudo (Esc) divided into 100 centavos. Esc 1,000 = 1 Conto. The Mozambique escudo is equivalent in value to, but not freely convertible with the Portuguese escudo. The following denominations are in circulation:

Notes: 50, 100, 500 and 1,000 escudos
(issued by the Banco Nacional Ultramarino)
Copper, nickel
and silver coins: 10, 20 and 50 centavos; 1, 2½, 5, 10 and
20 escudos

South African currency is widely accepted, but is not legal tender.

Niger

The same regulations apply to Niger as the Ivory Coast. See Ivory Coast.

Nigeria

A currency declaration in duplicate is required both on arrival and on departure. The import or export of Nigerian currency of any denomination is prohibited.

The unit of currency is the naira which is divided into 100 kobo. One naira is equivalent to the old 10 shillings. The following denominations are in circulation:

Notes: 50 kobo; 1, 5, 10, 50 and 100 nair
Coins: ½, 1, 5, 10 and 25 kobo

Rhodesia

Visitors must have sufficient financial resources to cover the period of their proposed stay and onward journey.

There is no limit on the amount of money in cash or traveller's cheques that may be brought into the country. Cash should be declared to customs and a certificate obtained to ensure that the unspent balance can be taken out on departure.

The Rhodesian unit of currency is the dollar ($) divided into 100 cents.

The denominations in circulation are:

Notes: $10.00, $5.00, $2.00, $1.00
Silver coins: 25c, 20c, 10c, 5c, 2½c
Copper coins: 1c, ½c

Rwanda

Only RF5,000 may be taken into Rwanda and both residents and non-residents may take out only a similar amount. There is no restriction on the amount of foreign currency entering Rwanda, nor on the export of foreign currency by non-residents; residents must seek the permission of the Central Bank before exporting such currency.

The unit of currency is the franc (RF).

The denominations of the currency in circulation are:

Coins: 1, 5 and 10 francs
Notes: 20, 50, 100, 500 and 1,000 francs

The franc coins issued by the former Banque d'Emission du Ruanda Urundi (B.E.R.B.) are still legal tender and of the same value as the Banque du Rwanda franc.

Senegal

For Senegal regulations see notes on Mauritania.

South Africa

There is no upper limit to the amount of money a visitor may take into South Africa but he must be able to prove he has sufficient means to maintain himself (approx. £120 per month). On arrival visitors must complete special customs forms, listing all their hold-ings of currency, and a stamped copy is retained by them. On departure from the country, visitors are allowed to take out as much money as is shown on the customs form; application must be made to the South African Reserve Bank for permission to take out any money in excess of this amount.

The unit of currency is the rand (R) divided into 100 cents.
The following denominations are in circulation:

Notes: 1, 5, 10 and 20 rand
Nickel coins: 5, 10, 20 and 50 cents

Other coins in circulation are 2 cents, 1 cent and $\frac{1}{2}$ cent.
The South African Reserve Bank has the sole right to issue bank notes, which are legal tender in South Africa, South West Africa, and the independent states of Botswana, Lesotho and Swaziland.

Spanish Sahara

The unit of currency is the peseta (Pta) divided into 100 centimos.
The following denominations are in circulation:

Notes: 100, 500 and 1,000 pesetas
Coins: 1, 2.50, 5, 25, 50, 100 pesetas; 10 and 50 centimos

Sudan

Visitors to the Sudan must declare on a form obtainable at the point of entry, all currency and negotiable documents in their possession, and are required to account for these on departure. It is illegal to take Sudanese currency out of the country. The form must be endorsed whenever traveller's cheques or foreign currency are exchanged and must be presented to customs on departure.

The unit of currency is the Sudanese pound (£S) divided into 100 piastres (PT) and 1,000 milliemes (mms).

The following denominations are in circulation:

Notes: 1, 5 and 10 Sudanese pounds; 25 and 50 piastres
Coins: 2, 5 and 10 piastres; 1, 2, 5 and 10 milliemes

Tanzania

Tanzanian currency may not be taken into Tanzania or taken out on departure. This prohibition extends to Kenya and Uganda. Traveller's cheques of any value may be imported and exported provided that they are properly documented in the traveller's passport.

The unit of currency is the Tanzania shilling, which is divided into 100 cents.

The Tanzania shilling is at par with the Kenya and Uganda shillings.

Denominations of the currency in circulation are:

Notes: 5, 10, 20 and 100 shillings
Coins: 5, 20 and 50 cents; 1 and 5 shillings

Tchad

For Tchad regulations, see notes on Central African Republic.

Togo

For Togo regulations, see notes on Dahomey

Tunisia

Visitors are not allowed to take Tunisian currency into or out of the country. Travellers entering or leaving Tunisia with Tunisian currency in their possession will have it impounded.

There is no restriction on the amount of foreign currency which can be taken into the country.

Tunisian currency held in excess at the time of departure can only be exchanged back into foreign currency on production of exchange slips from Tunisian banks. The amount of excess currency exchanged back must not exceed 30 per cent of foreign currency originally exchanged, or 100 dinars, whichever is the greater.

The official unit of currency is the Tunisian dinar (D) divided into 1,000 millimes (m). The following denominations are in circulation:

Notes: ½, 1, 5 and 10 dinars
Coins: 1, 2, 5, 10, 20, 50, 100 and 500 millimes

Uganda

The currency issue is under the control of the Bank of Uganda, which levies a small charge on the exchange of sterling into Ugandan currency.

There is no restriction on the import of sterling either in notes or traveller's cheques, but the export of sterling is restricted to notes not exceeding the amount imported. Any amount of other East African currency notes may be imported from or exported to Kenya and Tanzania, but the import and export of Ugandan currency to other countries including Kenya and Tanzania is restricted. Travellers wishing to visit countries outside the sterling area from Uganda should arrange with their British bankers for foreign exchange facilities, or obtain an authority from the Bank of England for any foreign exchange facilities they expect to need in Uganda; banks in Uganda will honour an authority granted by the Bank of England.

The unit of currency is the Uganda shilling, divided into 100 cents. Denominations of currency in circulation are:

Notes: 5, 10, 20 and 100 shillings
Coins: 5, 10, 20 and 50 cents; 1 and 2 shillings

Zaire

The National Bank's 1972 exchange control regulations place a complete embargo on the export or import of Zairian bank notes by residents or non-residents alike, but there is no limit on the amount of foreign currency that visitors may bring into or take out of the country. On arrival, all visitors are required to fill in a currency declaration form (serial No. DM 1) which also serves as a record of all currency exchange effected during the course of the visit to Zaire, and the duplicate copy of the form has to be surrendered to the National Bank representative at the place of exit. As a normal rule, visitors are also required to show on leaving the country that they have spent not less than Z20 for each day of the visit. (Principal exceptions are directors and other non-resident members of companies in Zaire whose costs are a proper charge to a local company, close relatives of persons resident in Zaire, technical personnel on contract to a local company, and in certain cases airline and shipping line personnel. Local companies may also be able to get a derogation from the National Bank for certain other categories of visitors.)

The unit of currency is the zaire (Z) made up of 100 makuta (K) (singular: Likuta); 1 likuta is the equivalent of 100 sengi. Denominations of the currency in circulation are:

Notes: 10, 20 and 50 makuta; 1 and 5 zaire
Coins: 10 sengi, 1 likuta and 5 makuta

Zambia

A maximum of 10 kwacha in Zambian currency may be taken into or out of the country. Visitors are, therefore, advised to carry traveller's cheques in small denominations, and to cash only sufficient for their current needs.

Visitors may take into Zambia as much foreign currency as they wish but they can take out no more than the equivalent of 20 kwacha unless they produce a receipt to prove that they took it in with them. For visitors, there are no restrictions on the amount of traveller's cheques taken into or out of the country.

The unit of currency is the kwacha which is divided into 100 ngwee. Denominations of currency in circulation are:

Notes: 50 ngwee; 1, 2, 10 and 20 kwacha
Coins: 1, 2, 5, 10 and 20 ngwee

Part 7
Regulations and Information for Crossing the Sahara

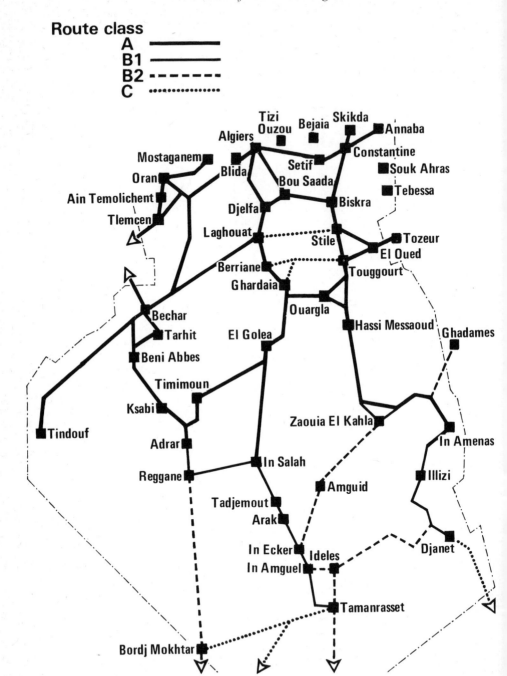

This diagrammatic map indicates the major road and track network in the Algerian Sahara. Many of the minor tracks and place-names are not shown.

Three North—South major routes across the Sahara

From Algiers. The RN1, the designated Trans-Saharan Highway, crosses the country passing through Djelfa, Laghouat, Ghardaia and El Golea to In Salah. The hard-surfaced road ends about 60 miles on from here and a track gives access to Tamanrasset and Agades in the Niger Republic.

An alternative route, the RN8 from Algiers to Djelfa, runs through Bou-Saada.

From Morocco. Coming via Saidia, Berkane, Oujda or Figuig, one can take the western Sahara route, the RN6, via Saidia and Ain Sefra towards Bechar, Abadla, Beni Abbes and Adrar. Here the hard-surfaced road ends and a track gives access to Reggane and the Tanezrouft region leading on to Gao in the Mali Republic.

The Trans-Saharan Highway route can be joined 40 miles south of El Golea by means of the tarred road via Timimoun (RN51) or by means of the track running from Reggane to In Salah via Aoulef (RN52).

The road from Bechar to Tindouf via Abadla (RN50) has now been completed and is tarmacadam-surfaced throughout.

From Tunisia. Coming from Tabarka or Ghardimaou one can take the eastern Sahara route, the RN3, which passes through Batna, Biskra, Touggourt, Ouargla, Hassi Messaoud and Hassi Bel Gueb-bour, at which point the road divides:

(a) There is a hard-surfaced road running from Hassi Bel Gueb-bour through Odjanet, Saut du Mouflon to In Amenas. The road then gives way to a track leading on to Illizi, Fort Gardel, Djanet and Le Djado and Faya Largeau in the Republic of Tchad.

(b) There is also a track linking Hassi Bel Guebbour to Amguid at which point the track divides into two further sections, one leading to Djanet, the second going on to Tamanrasset.

The Tozeur (Tunisia)—El Oued road has now been completed and gives quicker access to the Algerian south from Tunisia. The In Amenas—Ghadames road offers a modern link-up between neigh-bouring countries across southern Algeria.

Roads and Tracks

For motorists travelling on the northern Sahara roads and the tracks of central and southern Sahara, the routes are officially classified according to their practicability:

Class 'A' Routes. The following routes do not present any special difficulty: Laghouat—El Golea—In Salah (RN1); Ghardaia—Ouargla (RN49); Ouargla—Touggourt (RN3); Touggourt—El Oued (RN16) to Tozeur (Tunisia); Ouargla—Hassi Messaoud (RN49); Hassi Messaoud—Bel Guebbour—Mazoula—Tin Fouyé—In Amenas (RN3); El Oued—Stile (RN48); Bechar—Abadla—Adrar (RN6); Adrar—Timimoun—El Golea (RN6, RN51, RN1); Bechar—Abadla—Tindouf (tarred) (RN50); Bechar—Tarhit—Igli.

Class 'B' Routes. These call for special safety precautions. They are divided into the following two categories:

'B1': Tracks which are in fairly frequent use and are regularly maintained: Tadjmout—Arak—In Ecker—In Amguel—Tamanrasset (RN1); In Salah—Aoulef—Reggane (RN52); Adrar—Reggane (RN6); Hassi Bel Guebbour—Zaouia El Kahla (RN54); El Abed—Larache—Illizi—Djanet (RN3).

'B2': Seldom-used tracks with little or no maintenance: Reggane—Bordj Mokhtar to Gao (Mali) (RN6)*; Tamanrasset—Ghadames (Libya) (RN53); Zaouia El Kahla—Amguid—In Ecker (RN54); Zaouatanlaz—Ideles—In Amguel (RN55); Zaouatanlaz—Djanet (RN3); Tamanrasset—In Guezzam (RN1) to Agades (Republic of Niger).

(*Note: On these tracks there are three very difficult sections with risk of sand drifts at the 140 km, 350 km and 600 km markers.)

Class 'C' Routes. Conditions on these tracks are dangerous and traffic movement is restricted: Touggourt—Ghardaia via Guerrara; Guerrara—Berraine; Laghouat—Stile; Djanet to the Tchad frontier; Tamanrasset—Tin Zaouatene; Tamanrasset—Bordj Mokhtar; and all other tracks not listed in Class 'A' and 'B'.

A dig, lift and push operation in the southern Sahara desert, Algeria.

Travel Permits and Regulations

When on a 'B' class road or track, motorists should enquire about road conditions at the start of each section from the local authorities, town hall, police station, sub-prefecture or the local office of the 'Ponts et Chausses'.

Once the motorist has obtained this information he must obtain a travel permit from the local administrative office (town hall or sub-prefecture) at the departure point. The permit is only supplied after a declaration giving the following information:

Type and make of vehicle used.
Number of passengers and their identity.
Date and time of departure.
The next stopping place and the final destination.
The estimated date and time of arrival at the next stopping place taking into account the horse-power of the vehicle and prevailing road conditions.
The reason for the journey.

The travel permit will be supplied by the administrative authorities as they see fit on examination of the vehicle and an inspection of tyres and other equipment. On the journey the travel permit must be shown to police authorities on request.

Private vehicles may travel individually on Class 'B1' roads and tracks, but those travelling on a Class 'B2' road or track must form part of a convoy of at least two vehicles. Motorists must not stray from the roads or track. It is forbidden to drive at night on 'B2' roads and tracks.

Motorists are responsible for all search-party and breakdown charges incurred on Class 'B' roads and tracks, and travel at their own risk. The travel permit guarantees the necessary safety measures, but in no way holds the State responsible for any mishap.

Travel on Class 'C' tracks is permitted only by a Prefectural order defining the special safety precautions to be taken in addition to those for Class 'B' surfaces.

In the event of a breakdown, travellers must never move away from the vehicle.

Climatic Conditions

Travellers are strongly advised not to undertake a crossing of the Sahara during the period 1st June–September 15th, due to the prevailing conditions of intense heat and frequent sand storms. (Permission to travel can be refused.)

There is a considerable difference in day and night temperatures in the desert ranging on average from 100 F (36 C) during the day to 40 F (5 C) at night.

Due to the extremely dry climate and high temperatures all travellers crossing the Sahara should take in their luggage:

A moisturising face cream and vaseline for the lips.
Lemon or mint pastilles against the dryness and dust which cause sore throats; chewing gum is not advisable.
A 'cheche' (a muslin veil which the Saharans use to protect their heads) to give cover against the sirocco and sand storms.
Sunglasses, and a wide-brimmed hat to give cover against the sun.
Woollen clothing (pullovers, scarves), blankets and sleeping bags for protection during the cold nights.

Spending the night in an oasis

In the well-known oases there are 1–3 star hotels with restaurants. Some also have a swimming pool. (Showers can be rented at Tamanrasset, but water may only be available at certain times during the day.)

In the small oases there are huts or other Saharan resting points

A desert oasis on the Cairo to El Giza road, Egypt.

offering the very minimum of comfort. The only consolation is to be found in the natural beauty of the site. (Because of flies, it is advisable to camp in the desert, away from the oases.)

Watering Points

In the south Sahara, wells are very far apart and remain the main centres of habitation.

On the track leading from Adrar to Bordj Mokhtar on the Algerian border, drinking water can be found only at Reggane and Bordj Mokhtar. The first watering point in the Mali Republic is at Tessalit.

On the track leading from Tamanrasset to In Guezzam on the Algerian—Niger border water can only be found at In Guezzam itself. Across the border in the Niger Republic the watering points are at In Abbangarit and Arlit

Refuelling Points

Refuelling points have been installed along the main routes at the following localities:

Central route. El Golea, In Salah, Tadjmout, Tamanrasset, Arlit and Timimoun (RN51) linking the central and western routes.

Western route. Ain Sefra, Beni Onif, Bechar, Beni Abbes, Kerzag, Adrar, Reggane. Reports indicate that since the oil crisis supplies of fuel and lubricants are not now available between Adrar in Algeria and Mopti in Mali.

Eastern route. Hassi Messaoud, Hassi Bel Guebbour, In Amenas, Djanet, Amguid (RN4) linking the eastern and central routes.

Local Formalities and Customs

Custom and police formalities for those leaving Algeria by the Adrar—Goa track or El Golea—Agades route take place at the following points:

On Adrar—Goa route, at the Prefecture of Adrar.
Southbound on the El Golea—Agades route at Tamanrasset; only a passport and inoculations check is made at the In Guezzam Military Post.
Northbound in reverse order.

The documents usually required are a valid passport, vaccination certificate (smallpox and yellow fever), international driving licence, the logbook delivered by the country of origin and car insurance papers.

Travellers needing a visa to enter Algeria, and those who mean to travel in neighbouring Saharan countries before returning to Algeria, should make certain the visa is valid before leaving Algeria.

If the visa is due to expire whilst the traveller is out of Algeria, he should have the validity extended before he leaves Algeria. This can be done at the Prefecture of Algiers, Oran or Constantine.

Visas for entry into Mali or Niger are obtainable from the respective Embassies in the country of departure or at the Mali Embassy, Algiers or the Niger Embassy, Algiers.

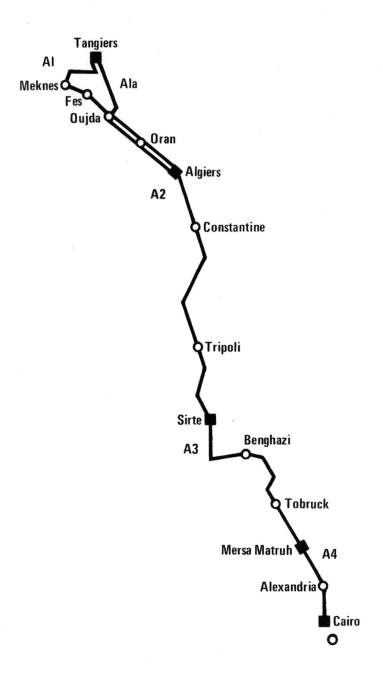

Tangiers

Al

Meknes

Ala

Fes

Oujda

Oran

Algiers

A2

Constantine

Tripoli

Sirte

Benghazi

A3

Tobruck

Mersa Matruh

A4

Alexandria

Cairo

Part 8
North Africa: West—East
Routes and Information

Trunk Routes		km	mls
A1	Tangiers—Algiers	1329	826½
A2	Algiers—Sirte	1777	1104½
A3	Sirte—Mersa Matruh	1386	861
	Special Note: authorised routes through Egypt		
	Special Note: ferry service between Egypt and Sudan		
A4	Mersa Matruh—Cairo	514	319½
	Total:	5006	3111½

Alternative Route			
A1a	Tangiers—Algiers	1278	793½

A1

TANGIERS	Trunk Route ⟱	CAIRO

⟱

Excellent all-weather tarred road passing through the picturesque Rif Mountains, via Larache on the Atlantic coast, Souk el Arba du Rharb and Sidi Kacem. Meknes all facilities, petrol plentiful.

267 km (166 mls)

MEKNES

Excellent all-weather tarred road via Fes through the Atlas Mountains, sinuous and picturesque, passing through several ravines

404 km (251 mls)

OUJDA
MOROCCO
+ + + + + +
ALGERIA

Good all-weather tarred road, fairly hilly passing over picturesque plain and hilly country. Report to Moroccan/Algerian police/customs control at frontier on leaving Oujda. Algerians insist on insurance being bought at frontier (in Algerian francs). Continue via Tlemcen and Ain Temouchent.

223 km (138 mls)

ORAN

Good tarred road throughout via Relizane, El Asnam, Khemis Miliana and Blida. Some hilly sections, a scenic route with fine views. Petrol plentiful.

435 km (270½ mls)

ALGIERS

Total: 1329 km (826½ mls)

A2

ALGIERS	Trunk Route ⇨	CAIRO
⬇	All-weather tarred road, crossing undulating wooded and hilly countryside. 445 km (276½ mls)	
CONSTAN-TINE	Good tarred road passing over hilly country-side; latter section has some sharp bends through the Tebessa mountains. 204 km (127 mls)	
TEBESSA ALGERIA + + + + + + TUNISIA	Good tar-surfaced road to frontier at Bou Chebka. Report to Algerian/Tunisian police/customs post. Road continues via Gafsa through semi-desert. 306 km (190 mls)	
GABES TUNISIA + + + + + + LIBYA	Good tar-surfaced road to frontier at Ras Jedir. Report to Tunisian/Libyan police/customs post. As a result of regulations issued by the Libyan Government, the Libyan Embassy in London will not issue visas for Libya if the holder's particulars are not in Arabic language. Road passes through semi-desert countryside. 349 km (217 mls)	
TRIPOLI	Good tarred road throughout passing at first through undulating cultivated countryside to Misurata via Leptis Magna. Continuing through mainly desert to Sirte with few facilities. 473 km (294 mls)	
SIRTE	Total: 1777 km (1104½ mls)	

SIRTE	Trunk Route ▷	CAIRO

SIRTE ⬇

Good tarred road throughout passing through desert with no settled population except in a few villages. Petrol available at Ben Gawad, Marble Arch, Ajedabya and Chemines. Extra petrol and water should be carried. Beware of sand drifts on the road, especially at night. Accommodation very limited.

570 km (354 mls)

BENGHAZI

Good tarred road throughout passing through scrub country and across the edge of the Jebel Akhdar Plateau. All facilities at Derna; road passes Knightsbridge Cemetery (I.W.G.C.)

458 km (284½ mls)

TOBRUCK

LIBYA
++++++
EGYPT

Good tarred road passing over desert plateau coastal plain and low undulating hills. Report to Libyan police/customs at Um Sa'ad on frontier and to Egyptian police/customs at Soloum. Allow at least three hours for immigration and customs processing, also fixing of temporary Egyptian number plates. Tarred road continues from frontier through desert countryside.

358 km (22½ mls)

Important note: due to the present Arab/Israeli confrontation, permission must be obtained to travel within Egypt (see p. 86). The latest information on areas open to foreigners is given on the following page.

MERSA MATRUH

Total: 1386 km (861 mls)

Special Note: authorised routes through Egypt

The Egyptian authorities have announced that the following areas are now open to foreigners visiting the country with a motor vehicle:

The coastal road from Soloum on the Egyptian/Libyan frontier to Alexandria (Gate 5)

The principal towns in the Suez Canal area via the following routes:

(a) Port Said: Via the Cairo—Benha—El Mansura—Damietta (Dumyat) road.

(b) Ismailiya: via the Delta agricultural road.

(c) Suez: via the desert road.

The following areas are closed to foreigners:

The Red Sea area south of the town of Suez to the Egyptian/Sudanese frontier.

The zone south of Soloum to the Egyptian frontier.

The El Mukattam district in Cairo.

The Aswan Dam area.

The side roads in the Delta area, including the Zifta—Mit Ghamr road.

Special Note: ferry service between Egypt and the Sudan

The steamer *Ten Ramadan* came into service on 1st May 1975 and sails between the Aswan High Dam, Egypt and Wadi Halfa, Sudan, departing on Thursday and returning the following Wednesday.

Capacity
First class: 32 passengers
Second class: 44 passengers
Third class: 190 passengers

A barge attached to the steamer accommodates 500 third-class passengers and can also carry motor vehicles.

Tickets issued by the Cairo and Aswan offices should be bought in Egyptian currency, and those issued by the Khartoum and Wadi Halfa offices in Sudanese currency.

Passenger rates
First class: £E10 (Egyptian pounds)
Second class: £E7.50
Third class: £E3
(Children between the ages of 4 and 12 years pay half-fare.)

Car rates
Average: £E35
Station wagon type: £E45

Travellers intending to use this service should first read the notes concerning the issue of visas and motoring permits in the Sudan (page 35, and pages 229–232).

MERSA MATRUH	**Trunk Route** ⇨	**CAIRO**

⇩

Asphalt road in fair condition passing over flat barren countryside.

291 km (181 mls)

ALEX-ANDRIA

There are two routes, the express way through the Nile Delta (138½ mls), or the desert route via Amriah and the Pyramids. The former route may be closed due to security precautions.

223 km (138½ mls)

CAIRO

Total: 514 km (319½ mls)

A1a

TANGIERS	Alternative Route ⇨	ALGIERS

⬇

A picturesque road along the high ridge of the Rif Range and descending to the Hoceima Plain, undulating with many hairpin bends. Road liable to be blocked by snow from December to April between Bab Taza and Targuist. Altitude of passes – Bab Besen 5000 ft, Bab Tizichen 5184 ft and Targuist Pass 3773 ft. Asphalt road throughout with some uneven stretches between Derdara and Targuist.

327 km (203 mls)

AL HOCEIMA

Good asphalt road ascending by hairpin bends through the beautiful valley of the Oued Nekor to the summit of the Neker Massif and descending into and across the Plain of Gareb. Road continues, skirting the edge of the Beni Iznassen Massif.

293 km (182 mls)

OUJDA

MOROCCO
+ + + + + +
ALGERIA

Good all-weather tarred road, fairly hilly passing over picturesque plain. Report to Moroccan/Algerian police/customs control at frontier on leaving Oujda. Algerians insist on insurance being bought at frontier (in Algerian francs). Continue via Tlemcen and Ain Temouchent.

223 km (138 mls)

ORAN

Good tarred road throughout via Relizane, El Asnam, Khemis Miliana and Blida. Some hilly sections, a scenic route with fine views. Petrol plentiful.

435 km (270½ mls)

ALGIERS	Total: 1278 km (793½ mls)

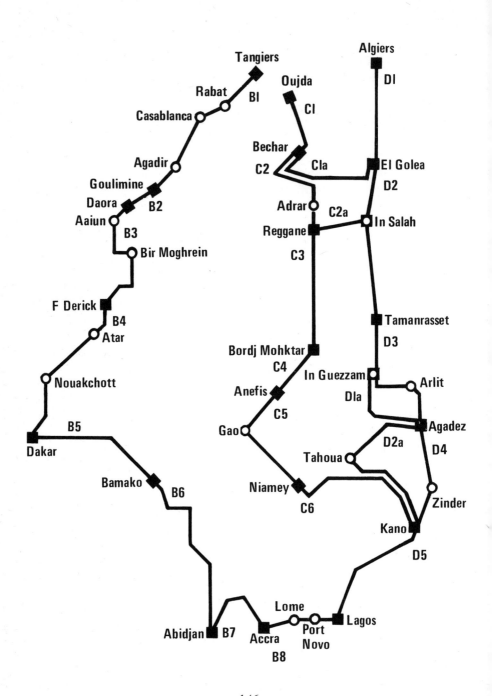

Part 9
West Africa: North—South Routes and Information

Trunk Routes		km	mls
B1	Tangiers—Goulimine	1104	686
B2	Goulimine—Daora	480	298
B3	Daora—F'Derick	791	491
B4	F'Derick—Dakar	1362	845
B5	Dakar—Bamako	1250	776
B6	Bamako—Abidjan	1181	734½
B7	Abidjan—Accra	830	516
B8	Accra—Lagos	495	307½
	Total:	7493	4654
C1	Oujda—Bechar	491	304½
C2	Bechar—Reggane	719	446½
C3	Reggane—Bordj Mohktar	628	391
C4	Bordj Mohktar—Anefis	438	272
C5	Anefis—Niamey	656	423
C6	Niamey—Kano	962	598
	Total:	3894	2435

Alternative Routes

C1a	Bechar—El Golea	1012	629
C2a	Reggane—In Salah	287	178

Trunk Routes

D1	Algiers—El Golea	891	554
D2	El Golea—Tamanrasset	1104	686
D3	Tamanrasset—Agadez	917	571
D4	Agadez—Kano	732	455
D5	Kano—Lagos	1126	708½
	Total:	4770	2974½

Alternative Routes

D1a	In Guezzam—Agadez	481	299
D2a	Agadez—Kano	1065	662

B1

TANGIERS	Trunk Route ⇨	DAKAR
⇩		
	Fairly level fast coastal route to Asilah continuing across undulating countryside to Larache, Kenitra and Rabat. Excellent tarmac road throughout. 286 km (178 mls)	
RABAT	Excellent fast motorway. 93 km (58 mls)	
CASA- BLANCA	Good tarmac road throughout, across cultivated countryside. 351 km (218 mls)	
ESSAOUIRA	Hilly road, good tar surfaces with some dangerous bends approaching Agadir along a fine corniche. 172 km (107 mls)	
AGADIR	Fairly good hard-surfaced road throughout. *Important note:* The route south of Goulimine should not be used by the inexperienced desert traveller, as some sections are most difficult to negotiate without four-wheel drive supported by adequate unsanding equipment. It is extremely hazardous and is not recommended. A compass and binoculars should be carried as an aid to navigation. 202 km (126 mls)	
GOULI- MINE	**Total: 1104 km (686 mls)**	

GOULI-MINE

Trunk Route ⇨	DAKAR

⇩

Single-width tar road for 90 km (56 mls), poor conditions. Improved gravel for 40 km (25 mls), last 15 km (9 mls) single-width tar. Road generally poor and liable to flooding on last section. Petrol should be available in Tan Tan: fill up as none until Aaiun. Report to police for stamp.

145 km (90 mls)

TAN TAN

Road tarred. Hotel at beach.

25 km (15½ mls)

TAN TAN PLAGE

Very bad conditions; maximum speed 20 kph (12½ mph); track is mostly large flints interspersed with areas of soft sand. Absence of markers makes navigation tricky. Compass needed. At Tarfaya police control, have documents stamped to cross Moroccan/Spanish Sahara border.

235 km (146 mls)

TARFAYA

MOROCCO
+ + + + + +
SPANISH
SAHARA

Poor earth track; maximum speed 20 kph (12½ mph). Moroccan frontier post/customs.

30 km (18½ mls)

TAH

Road tarred to 10 ft wide but worn down and in poor condition. Maximum speed 30–35 kph (18–22 mph). Police/customs control at Daora off main track near military airfield must be visited to have documents stamped. To miss, will incur heavy fine.

45 km (28 mls)

DAORA

Total: 480 km (298 mls)

| **DAORA** | **Trunk Route** ⬇ | **DAKAR** |

Road tarred to 10 ft wide in fair condition, maximum speed 40 kph (25 mph). Police control at Aaiun. Petrol and water available also at Parador (hotel).

40 km (25 mls)

AAIUN

Road tarred 10 ft wide, fair condition. Maximum speed 45 kph (28 mph). Bu Craa military camp 2 km to side of road.

120 km (74½ mls)

BU CRAA

First 15 km (9 mls) good tarred surface. Remaining 125 km (77½ mls) fair gravel track, maximum speed 35 kph (22 mph). Petrol and police control/customs at Guelta Zemmur.

140 km (87 mls)

GUELTA ZEMMUR
SPANISH
SAHARA
++++++
MAURITANIA

First 16 km (10 mls) tar surface 10 ft wide; remaining 74 km (46 mls) improved gravel across Spanish Sahara/Mauritania frontier. Report to police control/customs at Bir Moghrein.

90 km (56 mls)

BIR MOGHREIN

Good track for 350 km (217½ mls); next 51 km (31½ mls) less well marked. At 236 km (146½ mls) sign indicates tropics 24° lat. The Sebkas are not visible from the track. Police control at F'Derick: report. Petrol and hotel available. (Zouerate 3 km (2 mls) east on an excellent tar road.)

401 km (248½ mls)

| **F'DERICK** | **Total: 791 km (491 mls)** |

F'DERICK	Trunk Route ⇨	DAKAR

⇩

Track very sandy and difficult in places. Maximum speed is restricted to 32 kph (20 mph). Track appears to cross Spanish Sahara border 30 km (18½ mls) north of Agui, re-entering and crossing railway line. From Agui the track continues south over flat sand and gravel for 45 km (28 mls) and then 53 km (32 mls) over mountains through Timzac Pass to Atar. Report to police. Petrol available.

304 km (189 mls)

ATAR

Fair to good gravel track 20 ft wide, maximum speed 70 kph (43 mph); 2-lane all-weather tarmac last 80 km (50 mls) to Nouakchott, capital of Mauritania. All facilities.

473 km (293 mls)

NOUAK-CHOTT
MAURITANIA
+ + + + + +
SENEGAL

Good tarmac 2-lane road. Liable to flood in wet season. Ferry available to cross river Senegal. Report to police control/customs.

214 km (133 mls)

RICHARD TOLL

From ferry, report to police/customs control at Richard Toll, 21 km (13 mls) from landing stage. All facilities.
Good all-weather tarred road to St. Louis. All facilities.

103 km (64 mls)

ST LOUIS

Excellent tarred road throughout, over picturesque countryside. Petrol available at Louga 75 km (46½ mls), Mekhe 150 km (93 mls) and at Thies 198 km (123 mls). Dakar all facilities.

268 km (166 mls)

DAKAR

Total: 1362 km (845 mls)

DAKAR	Trunk Route ⇨	LAGOS

⇩

Good all-weather tar road to Maleme Hodar 298 km (185 mls). Remaining 157 km (98 mls) improved gravel, may become impassable during rainy season. All rivers bridged. Tambacounda all facilities. Longest distance between petrol points 75 km (46 mls)

455 km (282 mls)

TAMBA-COUNDA

SENEGAL
+ + + + + +
MALI

Partially improved road to Goudiry 113 km (70 mls) continuing earth road to Nahe 67 km (41½ mls). Senegal/Mali border: police/customs control.
Ferry across river at Kidira, earth road for 105 km (65 mls) to Kayes police/customs control. All facilities. Route very difficult to all vehicles other than 4-wheel drive, very sandy, impassable between June and November. Vehicles can be railed from Dakar or Tambacounda; a check should always be made at the latter to ensure that the ferry at Kidira is in working order.

285 km (177 mls)

KAYES

Untarred cross-country track only suitable for 4-wheel drive vehicles. Beware of soft sand, becomes impassable between June and November. Vehicles can be railed. Petrol and water available at Toukoto and Kita. Motorised ferry at Bafoulabe, maximum load 15 metric tons.

510 km (317 mls)

BAMAKO	Total: 1250 km (776 mls)

BAMAKO	Trunk Route ⇨	LAGOS

⬇

Good all-weather tar road throughout with all rivers bridged. Petrol available at Bougouni and Sikasso. Report to police/customs control at Zegoua.

474 km (295 mls)

ZEGOUA
MALI
+ + + + + +
IVORY COAST

From Zegoua cross Mali/Ivory Coast frontier on improved laterite and gravel road, passing through dry savanna countryside. Petrol available at Nielle and Ouangolodougou. Report to police/customs control at Ferkessedougou. All facilities.

141 km (88 mls)

FERKESS-EDOUGOU

Improved laterite and gravel road, untarred. Surface bad in places especially in rainy season between Niakaramandougou and Katiola. Petrol at Tafire and Niakaramandougou.

240 km (149 mls)

BOUAKE

Good all-weather tar road throughout. Petrol available at Tiebissou, Toumodi, Tiassale, Sikensi and Dabou. All facilities at Abidjan, capital of Ivory Coast.

326 km (202½ mls)

ABIDJAN	Total: 1181 km (734½ mls)

ABIDJAN	Trunk Route ⇨	LAGOS
⬇		
	Good all-weather tar road through thick rain forests. All rivers bridged. Petrol available at Anyama, Adzope and Akoupe. 214 km (133 mls)	
ABEN-GOUROU	Good tar road to Agnibilerou 70 km (43½ mls). Remainder only partially improved laterite and gravel with some poor sections. Report to police/customs control at Takikroum. 105 km (65 mls)	
TAKIKROUM IVORY COAST + + + + + + GHANA	Partially improved laterite and gravel road with some poor sections. Report to police/customs control at Dormaa-Ahenkro. Petrol available. 70 km (44 mls)	
BEREKUM	Good tar road through savanna to Kumasi 161 km (100 mls), all facilities available. Continues tar through tropical rain forest to capital Accra 280 km (174 mls). All facilities. Petrol available at Sunyani, Nkawkaw, Kibi and Nsawam. 441 km (274 mls)	
ACCRA	Total: 830 km (516 mls)	

Tar ■ ■ **Gravel** ⠿ **Earth** ⹀ **Desert** | **B8**

| ACCRA | Trunk Route ⇨ | LAGOS |

⇩

GHANA
+ + + + + +
TOGO

All-weather tarred road throughout. Toll at Sogakope. Report to police/customs control at Denu on leaving Ghana and at Aflao on entering Togo. Lome all facilities.
210 km (125 mls)

LOME

A tarred all-weather road passing through three countries, Togo, Dahomey and Nigeria. Report to police/customs controls at borders in Condji, Igolo and Idiroko. Petrol available throughout. All facilities Lagos.
294 km (182½ mls)

TOGO
+ + + + + +
DAHOMEY

DAHOMEY
+ + + + + +
NIGERIA

LAGOS Total: 495 km (307½ mls)

C1

OUJDA	Trunk Route ⇨	KANO

⇩

Good asphalt road throughout passing over the Col de Jerada and through undulating wooded countryside which becomes increasingly drier and more desert-like towards Tenrara. The road is liable to flash floods at a number of places before and after Bouarfa during heavy falls of rain in the area. Petrol available at Tenrara. On arrival Figuig, report to police control immigration and customs. All facilities available at Figuig.

376 km (233½ mls)

FIGUIG

MOROCCO
+ + + + + +
ALGERIA

Good asphalt road continues passing through fairly flat desert countryside. Cross Moroccan/Algerian frontier at Zenaga 5 km (3 mls) from Figuig and report to police/immigration/customs at Beni-Ounif after a further 4 km. Beware of loose sand on road. All facilities at Bechar.

115 km (71 mls)

BECHAR

Total: 491 km (304½ mls)

BECHAR	**Trunk Route** ⇩	**KANO**

Good asphalt road continues; beware of loose sand on road. Some sections of road liable to flood after heavy rain. Petrol available at Beni Abbes 240 km (149 mls), Kersaz 348 km (216 mls) and Ksabi 426 km (265 mls). Petrol reserve should be carried in case it is not available at any of the places. End of asphalt road at Adrar where all facilities available. Report to police control.

585 km (363½ mls)

ADRAR

Tanezrouft route begins: category B2 track. Report to police control and customs. Journey can only be continued in a convoy; a 'Carte d'Embarquement' has to be filled in and you may have to wait for other vehicles to make up convoy.

(*Note:* Offices close at 12.00 noon Saturday for the weekend and on Moslem festivals. For regulations governing movements en route see Part 7, page 131.)

Leave Adrar on Palmerie route – it is essential to ask the way as there appear to be no signposts out of town and there are two tracks. Fairly hard dirt track throughout with corrugations close together. All facilities at Reggane. Report to police control. (For route to In Salah see Branch Route C2a.)

134 km (83 mls)

REGGANE

Total: 719 km (446½ mls)

REGGANE	Trunk Route ⇨	**KANO**

⬇

	Leave as for Mali. Desert track throughout, with sandy patches, bumps, rocky ridges and corrugations. Navigational aids; small survey beacons every 5 km, old oil drums at irregular intervals and Berliet type marking (poles with rectangular tops). Route passes through fairly flat countryside with low sand dunes, average speed 48–64 kph (30–40 mph). Poste Weygand, deserted, comprises ruined shed and four old nissen huts. No facilities. 250 km (156 mls)
POSTE WEYGAND	Desert track throughout with sandy patches, bumps, stony surfaces, rocky ridges and corrugations, flanked by sand dunes. Navigational aids as before. Route crosses Tropic of Cancer (sign board) 132 km (82 mls) and through Bidon V 259 km (161 mls), derelict staging post containing two metal towers and remains of huts and water cisterns. Average speed 48–64 kph (30–40 mph). Fairly flat countryside. Algerian frontier post and military fort at Bordj Mohktar. Report to police. Water available (not very good) pumped from well. 378 km (235 mls)
BORDJ MOHKTAR	Total: 628 km (391 mls)

BORDJ MOHKTAR	Trunk Route ⇨	KANO

⬇

ALGERIA
++++++
MALI

Track to frontier bears right to a S.E. direction, after about 8 mls; follow bed of Wadi for another 8 mls, pass Lone Tree and after about 3 mls a line of trees along Wadi to Algeria/Mali border. Track bumpy and sandy. Border marked by unmarked slab of masonry by roadside. Track curves west, then south and is sandy with corrugations. Adrar Des Iforhas hills in sight ahead. Deviation around military camp and airstrip about 8 mls before Tessalit. Report to police control and customs on arrival. Offices closed from 12.00 hrs – 15.00 hrs. Water available.

153 km (95 mls)

TESSALIT

Route passes through slag hill type hills undulating on sandy, dusty, twisting, badly corrugated track, passing over a number of bridges over dry wadis. Aguelhok, small village after 96 km (60 mls). Anefis, small village, report to military control post.

285 km (177 mls)

ANEFIS

Total: 438 km (272 mls)

ANEFIS	**Trunk Route** ⇨	**KANO**

GAO

Track continues on featureless flat desert passing Monument Chudeau after 6 mls. Small scattered village of Tabankort with many deep wells after a further 9 mls, track branches here and the one to the left should be taken for Gao. Ruined mud fort passed on the left of track which continues with a series of deep sandy patches and corrugations passing flat topped hills on the left horizon. At Gao report to police station; two or three passport photos must be produced if photographic permit required. This is obligatory in Mali. All facilities available.

213 km (148 mls)

■ MALI
+ + + + + +
■ NIGER

Ensure that you leave with sufficient stocks of petrol for the journey. Dirt and improved gravel road following on the bank of the Niger River. Dirt-surfaced with improved gravel sections and sealed towards Niamey. Some pot-holes and corrugations will be encountered. Mali customs at Labezanga and Niger customs at Ayorou. All facilities at Niamey. Report to police control.

443 km (275 mls)

NIAMEY

Total: 656 km (423 mls)

NIAMEY	Trunk Route ⬦	KANO

	A sealed tarmac road for 140 km (87 mls) to Dosso where it continues to Birni Nkonni on improved gravel-surfaced road with some rough corrugated sections. 422 km (262 mls)	
BIRNI NKONNI	Improved gravel-surfaced road to Madaoua for 88 km (55 mls) then a smooth fast tarmac road to Maradi. 315 km (196 mls)	
MARADI NIGER + + + + + + NIGERIA	A smooth road throughout. Report to Niger customs at Dan Issa; cross Niger/Nigeria border and report to Nigerian customs at Jibiya. All facilities at Kano. 225 km (140 mls)	
KANO	**Total: 962 km (598 mls)**	

BECHAR	Alternative Route ⟰	**EL GOLEA**

⟱

BENI ABBES

Good asphalt road throughout passing over flat desert with small sand dunes: beware of loose sand on road. Some sections before Timimoun liable to flood after heavy rain. Petrol available at Beni Abbes 240 km (149 mls), Kersaz 348 km (216 mls), Ksabi 426 km (264 mls), and Timimoun 652 km (405 mls). All facilities at El Golea.

KERZAZ

KSABI

TIMIMOUN

EL GOLEA   Total: 1012 km (629 mls)

■■■ Tar ■ ■ Gravel ⸬⸬ Earth ══ Desert	**C2a**

REGGANE	Alternative Route ⇨	**IN SALAH**

⇩

Large sign-post pointing left to Algiers and right to Mali. Proceed right for 100 yds to police post for authorisation and filling in of forms for onward journey. Return to sign-post and leave left for Algiers. Fairly flat partially improved, dusty, dirt and gravel track, marked by beacons/cairns passing through the undulating Plaine du Tidikelt, corrugated and potholed in places. Beware of drifting sand. Track splits into three after Aoulef, be sure to take correct one. Carry extra fuel and water on this section.

IN SALAH	**Total: 287 km (178 mls)**

D1

ALGIERS	Trunk Route ⇩	KANO

Class 'A' road. Good surface, tarred throughout. Two mountain ranges are crossed, the northern one, through the Chiffa Gorges and over the Atlas Mountains with a 3,000 ft escarpment between Blida and Berrouaghia, is slow going. Transport hotel at Berrouaghia. The second range is in the Ouled Nail Mountains, 4,300 ft on the Col Des Caravanes. Road enters the desert at Sidi-Maklouf. Beware of drifting sand on road. Laghouat has hotel and all facilities; fill up with petrol as prices may increase further south. Road sometimes affected by flooding in spring.

429 km (266½ mls)

LAGHOUAT

Class 'A' road. Good surface, tarred throughout, but beware of drifting sands across road. Between Tilrhemt and Berriane, road crosses several wadis which flood in winter. Military barracks, police and petrol at Ghardaia 191 km (119 mls) also camp site. No more petrol till El Golea, so fill up.

462 km (287 mls)

EL GOLEA

Total: 891 km (554 mls)

EL GOLEA	**Trunk Route** ⇨	**KANO**

Class 'B' road. Good tarred road over the Tademait Plateau and continues to In Salah. Route passes Fort Miribel which is now deserted; water is available at the Fort and 80 km (50 mls) further on at Tabaloulet. Well 220 yds east of the track. Well also at Ain el Hadjadj, east of the track which descends the Plateau, gradient 1-in-5. Do not depend on wells for water as it may not be available. Carry sufficient supplies. Report arrival and departure to police/military commandant in In Salah. All facilities.

410 km (255 mls)

IN SALAH

Class 'B1' road. First 96·5 km (60 mls) good tarred road then unsurfaced track, surface harder with corrugations spaced wider apart with less drifting sand. Arak Oasis and Gorges, beginning of ascent through the Mouydir Mountains, small sections of tarred road will be found after In Ecker and before Tamanrasset. Report arrival and departure to police/military commandant. Clear customs and have documents and passports stamped for exit and check currency. Fill up with fuel and water as supplies may not be available until Agadez.

694 km (431 mls)

TAMAN-RASSET

Total: 1104 km (686 mls)

■■■ Tar ■ ■ Gravel ⋯⋯ Earth ═ ═ Desert | **D3**

TAMAN-RASSET	**Trunk Route** ⇨	**KANO**

⇩

	Class 'B2' road: This is a most dangerous section, track not well defined, navigational care very necessary as track constantly changing to follow those made by other vehicles going off the main route. Beacons/cairns/ metal poles at 2 km distance: these signs must be strictly followed. Soft sand encountered before In Guezzam, when in doubt of surface recce on foot. Best time to travel is in early morning when sand is firmest. Do not get into lorry tracks. Report to post for passport check, also report arrival and departure to police in In Guezzam. Fill up with water and fuel if latter available.
	416 km (258½ mls)
IN GUEZZAM ALGERIA + + + + + + NIGER	Class 'B2' road: Route across desert to Assamaka 26 km (16 mls) of difficult soft sand. Route to Arlit well marked by posts approximately 2 km apart but extensive detours around wandering dunes may be expected. As long as one returns to the line of the markers after detours one should not get lost. Binoculars necessary here. Mileages are only approximate. All facilities at Arlit.
	221 km (138 mls)
ARLIT	Well defined desert track, surfaces sandy and heavily corrugated in places. Care should be taken. All facilities in Agadez. Report to police control on arrival.
	280 km (174½ mls)
AGADEZ	**Total: 917 km (571 mls)**

D4

AGADEZ	Trunk Route ⇩	KANO

Good 1- or 2-lane graded dirt road for first 64 km (40 mls). The next 193 km (120 mls) is very difficult going, requiring frequent 4-wheel drive over soft sand and bumps. It makes little difference if one attempts to drive right or left of the side of the track through the thorn bushes. Track improves 40 km (25 mls) north of Tanout and becomes fairly good but corrugated. After Tanout conditions are similar, surface more gravel than dirt. Report to police control at Zinder. All facilities.

471 km (292½ mls)

ZINDER

Tarred surface in fair to good condition. Niger customs at Matameye. Nigeria customs at Kongolam. Kano has all facilities.

261 km (162 mls)

NIGER

++++++

NIGERI

KANO

Total: 732 km (455 mls)

D5

KANO	Trunk Route ⇨	LAGOS
⇩		
	Good tarred all-weather road throughout via Zaria and Kaduna passing through high savanna country, petrol plentiful. All facilities at Kano. 561 km (348½ mls)	
KONTA-GORA	Good tarred all-weather road throughout, via Jebba, Ilorin, Ibadan and Shagamu. All rivers bridged, petrol plentiful. All facilities at Lagos. 565 km (360 mls)	
LAGOS	Total: 1126 km (708½ mls)	

Tar ■ ■ Gravel ⸬⸬⸬ Earth ═⹀═ Desert		**D1a**
IN GUEZZAM	Alternative Route ⟳	**KANO**

ALGERIA

++++++

NIGER

Class 'B2' road: Dangerous and difficult section. 29 km (18 mls) of flat sand to Niger border. Report to police/customs for formalities. Track continues through deep sand, 4-wheel drive frequently needed, surface also heavily corrugated restricting speed. 142 km (88 mls) south of In Guezzam track makes hairpin bend to north and then turns south again, take care it is not lost. Water available south of In Guezzam at 359 km (223 mls), 389 km (242 mls) and 438 km (272 mls). Report arrival and departure to police control Agadez. All facilities.

AGADEZ

Total: 481 km (299 mls)

		D2a
■■ Tar ■ ■ Gravel ⋯⋯ Earth ＝＝ Desert		

AGADEZ	Alternative Route ⇨	KANO
⬇		
	Track to In Waggeur in many places ill-defined, passing through and around thorn bushes. Improves after In Waggeur. Petrol available in Taboua. 449 km (279 mls)	
TAHOUA	Fairly fast good gravel road. After Kaloma road junction take right-hand route. No petrol at Madaoua. 165 km (102½ mls)	
MADAOUA	Good single-lane tarred road with hard shoulders. Expect occasional detours to avoid broken bridges. 226 km (140½ mls)	
MARADI NIGER + + + + + + NIGERIA	Tarred all-weather road. Niger customs at Dan Issa, Nigerian at Jibiya. 225 km (140 mls	
KANO		Total: 1065 (662 mls)

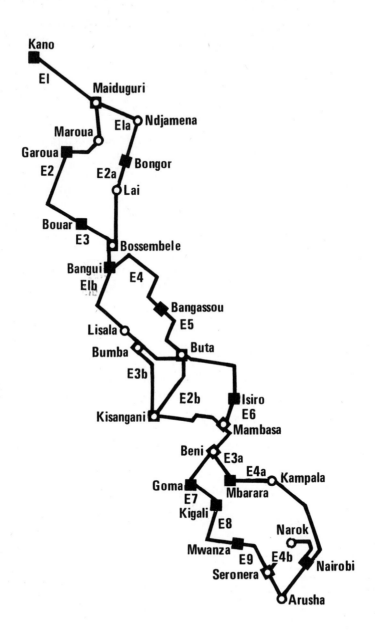

Kano

E1

Maiduguri

Ela Ndjamena

Maroua

Garoua

E2 E2a Bongor

Lai

Bouar

E3 Bossembele

Bangui

E1b E4

Bangassou

E5

Lisala Buta

Bumba

E3b

E2b Isiro

E6

Kisangani Mambasa

Beni E3a

E4a Kampala

Goma Mbarara

E7

Kigali E8

Narok

Mwanza E4b

E9 Seronera Nairobi

Arusha

Part 10
Central Africa: West—East Routes and Information

Trunk Routes		km	mls
E1	Kano—Garoua	1013	629
E2	Garoua—Bouar	719	447
E3	Bouar—Bangui via Bossembele	455	283
E4	Bangui—Bangassou	748	464
E5	Bangassou—Isiro via Buta	861	535
E6	Isiro—Goma	931	578½
E7	Goma—Kigali	181	112½
E8	Kigali—Mwanza	589	368½
E9	Mwanza—Nairobi via Seronera	909	565
	Special Note: information and service facilities		
	Total:	6406	3982½

Alternative Routes			
E1a	Maiduguri—Bongor	489	303
E2a	Bongor—Bossembele	746	460½
E3a	Beni—Mbarara	233	145
E4a	Mbarara—Nairobi	934	580

Branch Routes			
E1b	Bangui—Buta via Bumba	1195	742½
E2b	Buta—Mambasa via Kisangani	855	531½
E3b	Bumba—Kisangani	532	331
	Special Note: Kinshasa—Kisangani via Bangui (riverboat)		
E4b	Seronera—Nairobi	382	237

E1

KANO	Trunk Route ▷	NAIROBI

⬇

Good tarred road passing through undulating savanna to Maiduguri. Many potholes and crumbled edges on hard shoulder. Petrol at Potiskum and Damaturu. Maiduguri all facilities.

607 km (377 mls)

MAIDU-GURI

NIGERIA
+ + + + + +
CAMEROUN

Nigerian customs and immigration in Maiduguri. Good tarred road to Bama 69 km (43 mls) continuing a wide well-graded gravel road across the Cameroun frontier at Dar Jammal and on to Mora. Cameroun customs check 3–4 miles before Mora. Immigration at Mora, also petrol.

150 km (93 mls)

MORA

Fair/good gravel and earth road being improved, winding through picturesque hilly countryside, corrugated and potholed in places. It is advisable in wet weather to take the road via Meri through the hills to Maroua in order to by-pass any flooding in the low areas on the direct route. Road from Maroua onwards being improved, gravel surface, last 85 km (53 mls) is tarred, but in poor condition. Petrol available at Maroua and Garoua but extra should be carried over this section.

256 km (159 mls)

GAROUA

Total: 1013 km (629 mls)

GAROUA	**Trunk Route**	⬆	**NAIROBI**

All-seasons tarmac road passing through Benoue National Park. Elephant country. Picturesque wooded and hilly countryside. Extra petrol should be carried. Petrol and hotel at Ngaoundere.

293 km (182 mls)

NGAOUN-DERE

CAMEROUN

++++++

CENTRAL AFRICAN REPUBLIC

Dirt road with isolated patches of gravel, fair/good or clay. The road passes at first through hilly terrain. Cameroun/Central African frontier at Garoua Boulai. Report to police/immigration/customs. Extra petrol should be carried over this section.

267 km (166 mls)

GAROUA BOULAI

Good improved graded road, surface gravel and dirt, corrugated and potholed in places, passes through hilly countryside, some sharp curves. Petrol/customs/immigration at Bouar, also police check.

159 km (99 mls)

BOUAR

Total: 719 km (447 mls)

BOUAR	Trunk Route ⬦	**NAIROBI**

Road passes at first through hilly terrain, generally well aligned, although in places there are sharp curves. Surface is gravel or clay. There are some bridges to cross east of Bouar which should be approached with care. Petrol available at Yaloke 230 km (143 mls) and Bossembele. Advisable to carry extra.

298 km (185 mls)

BOSSEM-BELLE

Continuing hard dirt corrugated road to Yimibi, 13 km (8 mls) before Bangui. Report to police/customs check point. Petrol available. Join main tarmac for Bangui and report to police on arrival. This is important: do not take advice to the contrary. Be careful with cameras, see notes on photography (page 74). *Important*: Check on ferry at Bangassou as it is generally out of order. Alternative route via Zongo and Lisala, but not the best road conditions and not advised.

157 km (98 mls)

BANGUI	Total: 455 km (283 mls)

BANGUI	**Trunk Route** ⇨	**NAIROBI**
⇩		
	Good tar road to Sibut 185 km (115 mls), continuing good all-weather dirt-surface to Bambari. Petrol available at Damara, Sibut, Grimari and Bambari. 385 km (239 mls)	
BAMBARI	Narrow dirt road, fair surface potholed in places. Take care as livestock may be met on road. Petrol available at Alindad and Kembe. Bangassou has all facilities. Ferry generally out of order and river may only be crossed by raft made out of dugout canoes. Report arrival and departure to C.A.R. police/customs. (Expect to be asked to supply battery to start ferry if crossing into Zaire.) 363 km (225 mls)	
BANGAS-SOU	**Total: 748 km (464 mls)**	

E5

BANGAS-SOU	Trunk Route ⇨	NAIROBI

⬇

CENTRAL AFRICAN REPUBLIC +++++ ZAIRE	Cross river and report to Zaire police/customs at Ndu. Hard dirt road to Monga, potholed in places. Ferry over Uele at Bondo. Petrol available. This section of road badly pot-holed, also section to Buta. 404 km (251 mls)
BUTA	Hard dirt road, potholed and rough passing through bamboo archways. Take care on crude log bridges. Road improves on approaching Titule which has all facilities. 131 km (81 mls)
TITULE	The recommended route is via Bambili and Barambo to Poko. Road via Zobia very bad, red dirt with some potholes, but negotiable mostly in top gear. Deteriorates after Poko. Average 16 kph (10 mph). Isiro all facilities. Report to police. 326 km (203 mls)
ISIRO (PAULIS)	Total: 861 km (535 mls)

ISIRO (PAULIS)	**Trunk Route** ⇩	**NAIROBI**

⬇

Hard dirt road in poor condition, improves between Mungbere and Mambasa, take care during and after rainfall as road becomes very slippery. Petrol at Mambasa.

322 km (200 mls)

MAMBASA

Hard dirt road via Komanda in poor condition, take extra care during and after rainfall. Average speed 16 kph (10 mph) (down to 6 kph (4 mph) in places). Road improves on approach to Beni. No petrol.

219 km (136 mls)

BENI

Fair dirt road passing through Birunga National Park. No petrol available at Butembo, Lubero and Ruindi. The latter is a National Park camp site and departure point for visits to the park.

263 km (163½ ml)

RUINDI

Fair/good dirt road corrugated and bumpy in places. No petrol available at Rutshuru. Management Headquarters of Parks at Rumangabo. Report to police at Goma. All facilities. Clear immigration and customs on leaving.

127 km (79 mls)

GOMA

Total: 931 km (578½ mls)

GOMA	**Trunk Route** ⇨	**NAIROBI**

ZAIRE
+ + + + + +
RWANDA

Leave on tarmac road following shore of Lake Kivu and cross into Rwanda. At camp site Gisenyi, stringent security precautions needed against thieving. Report to police and clear immigration and customs. After leaving Gisenyi, road climbs up through the mountains to 8,202 ft and descends to Ruhengeri at 4,920 ft. The summit of the escarpment is reached after 35 km (22 mls). The road is winding, bumpy and dusty but very picturesque.

78 km (48½ mls)

RUHEN-GERI

Road continues to be very winding, steep, dusty, bumpy and very slow going. Average 24–32 kph (15–20 mph). No camp sites available due to intense agriculture. Missions at Rulindo and Temera. Petrol at Mugambazi. All facilities at Kigali. Report to police and clear customs and immigration before leaving for Tanzania. Stringent security precautions needed against thieving; camping illegal – see police for sites.

103 km (64 mls)

KIGALI

Total: 181 km (112½ mls)

KIGALI	Trunk Route ⇨	NAIROBI

At first a tarmac road leaving town, becoming a dusty gravel surface, winding through hilly countryside. Customs and immigration at Rusumu Falls. Cross River Kagera at Rusumu on new bridge.

170 km (105½ mls)

RUSUMU
RWANDA
+ + + + + +
TANZANIA

Military checkpoint in Tanzania after crossing bridge at Rusumu. Also customs and immigration. Continue on an improved dusty gravel road passing through hilly countryside to Rulenge, descending into plain. Water is scarce in this area and should be obtained from the petrol station in Biharamulo or the hospital.

171 km (109 mls)

BIHARA-MULO

Road reasonable but very dusty, corrugated and potholed in places. Cross estuary by toll ferry at Busisi, 14 km (9 mls) south of Mwanza, and continue on tarmac road. Allow half a day for this as ferry takes 20 minutes to cross and there are likely to be delays. Beware! Dress modestly, especially the ladies. All facilities.

248 km (154 mls)

MWANZA

Total: 589 km (368½ mls)

MWANZA	**Trunk Route** ⇨	**NAIROBI**

⬇

Tarmac road for 48–64 km (30–40 mls) from Mwanza, continuing on a fairly good dirt surface to the Ndabaka Gate into the Serengeti National Park. Road proceeds across the western corridor of the park which in wet weather is sometimes only possible with a 4-wheel drive vehicle. A fee of 20 shillings plus 10 shillings for the vehicle is payable on entering the park. A number of camp sites are available at Seronera, the Park Headquarters, for about 5 shillings a night. Petrol also available.

314 km (195 mls)

SERONERA

Fairly good, well-graded dusty dirt road, corrugated and potholed in sections to Ngorongoro. Improves to all-weather road with tarmac after Makuyuni to Arusha. All facilities at Arusha.

318 km (198 mls)

ARUSHA

TANZANIA
+ + + + + +
KENYA

All-weather road with tarmac throughout. Petrol available at Longido, Namanga, Bissel, Kajiado and Athi River. Tanzania frontier control/police/immigration at Longido. Kenya frontier control checkpoint at Namanga. Nairobi has all facilities.

277 km (172 mls)

NAIROBI

Total: 909 km (565 mls)

Special Note: information and service facilities

The Nairobi Information and Service Centre, organised by Messrs T. J. M. Bailey and P. J. Lewis, is situated on the Bahai Duck Farm, Kiamba Road (off Thika Road); tel: Nairobi 67447.

Travellers in need of information or advice on touring and onward travel, vehicle repairs, spares, etc., should contact Mr T. J. M. Bailey who is an expert in these matters. He may also be contacted through Bruce Travel Ltd, Koinange Street (opp. Post Office) or P.O. Box 40809; in his absence Mr P. J. Lewis may be contacted through Safari Camp Services (Nairobi's leading camp site), Simba Hill, Langatta (patron: D. Hodges); tel: Langatta 483 or P.O. Box 40809, Nairobi.

Information can be supplied on visas, purchase of provisions, spares, equipment, routes, road conditions, air flight arrangements, expeditions, safaris to Lake Rudolf, Mount Kenya and Olduwai Gorge, the Tanzanian and Ethiopian circuits, visiting and living with the Samburu people, etc. Telephone facilities are also availabe to overland company operators for contacting tour leaders in case of emergency.

The Service Centre has a fully equipped mechanical workshop with trained mechanics who specialise in the overhaul and repair problems overland travellers are likely to be presented with. Breakdown recovery, vehicle sales, car hire, and facilities for travellers to work on their own vehicles can also be arranged. Day and night watchmen provide maximum security.

E1a

MAIDU-GURI	Alternative Route ⇨	BOSSEM-BELE

⬇

NIGERIA + + + + + + CAMEROUN CAMEROUN + + + + + + TCHAD	Hard dirt road, corrugated with a few powdery patches, liable to become impassable for periods from Dikwa during the wet season, June–November. Report to Nigerian customs at Camboro, then cross bridge to Cameroun police and customs at Fotokol. Report to police/customs again on departure at Fort Foureau, turn half a mile to the right on the same side of the river to customs for ferry across confluence of Logone and Chari rivers to Ndjamena (Fort Lamy). Ferry closes at 17.30 hours. Toll. Report to Tchad police/customs on arrival. Fort Lamy has all facilities. 249 km (154 mls)
NDJAMENA (Fort Lamy)	Good tarmac road for 156 km (97 mls) to Guelengdeng, continuing hard dirt road to Bongor; this section is liable to close during rain storms: red and yellow barriers on road. Petrol at Bongor. 240 km (149 mls)
BONGOR	**Total: 489 km (303 mls)**

BONGOR	Alternative Route ⇨	**BOSSEM-BELE**

⬇

Hard dirt road, corrugated and potholed in places across flat plain parallel to river. Liable to be flooded and difficult in wet season. Petrol available at Lai and Doba.

265 km (164½ mls)

DOBA

Hard dirt road through scrub jungle hills. Very rough corrugations. Report to Tchad customs at Gore. Petrol.

100 km (62 mls)

GORE
TCHAD
++++++
CENTRAL
AFRICAN
REPUBLIC

Hard dirt corrugated road. Central African Republic customs post 24 km (15 mls) after leaving Gore. Petrol at Bossangoa. Report to police.

230 km (143 mls)

BOSSANGOA

Continuing hard dirt corrugated road. Petrol.

146 km (91 mls)

BOSSEM-BELE

Total: 746 km (460½ mls)

| Tar ■■ Gravel ⠿ Earth ＝ Desert | **E3a** |

| BENI | Alternative Route ⇨ | **NAIROBI** |

Very rough road to Uganda border descending through a vast valley and then climbing up to Kasindi. At 34 km (21 mls), junction for Mutwanga (distance 13 km (8 mls)) excursion base for climbing the Ruwenzori and for tours of the northern sector of the Mobutu Sese Seko Park. Report to police/customs at Kasindi.

80 km (50 mls)

KASINDI
ZAIRE
++++++
UGANDA

Hard dirt road. Uganda police/customs at Mpondwe. Continue through Queen Elizabeth Game Park via Katwe and Mweya on Lake Idi Amin Dada. Pay park fee and request permission to camp. Turn right and proceed south on tarmac, then hard dirt via Bushenyi. Animal life abundant.

153 km (95 mls)

MBARARA Total: 233 km (145 mls)

MBARARA	Alternative Route ⇨	**NAIROBI**

⇩

Good sealed road throughout via Masaka through interesting countryside, animal life abundant. Kampala has all facilities.

269 km (167 mls)

KAMPALA

Good hard tarmac road throughout. Petrol available at Jinja and Tororo.

211 km (131 mls)

TORORO

Good hard tarmac road through picturesque countryside. Uganda/Kenya customs at Malaba. Petrol available at all large towns. Nairobi has all facilities.

454 km (282 mls)

UGANDA
+ + + + + +
KENYA

NAIROBI

Total 934 km (580 mls)

BANGUI	Branch Route ▷	BUTA
⬇	*Note*: This alternative route is not advised unless undertaken with 4-wheel-drive vehicle. Cross river Oubangui by ferry and report to police/customs at Zongo. Ferry (toll), which takes 20 minutes. Allow 4 hours for customs. Hard narrow dirt road, at first, rutted and potholed surface, passing through tall jungle. Expect fallen trees across road after heavy rain. Average speed 24 kph (15 mph). Ferry at Bogilima efficient and free. Petrol not available on route so carry extra. 249 km (156 mls)	
GEMENA	Continuing dirt-surfaced road, with some very bad sand bars and ruts. More second-gear driving than third. Beware in wet weather as road can become inundated with water. Ferry (toll) at Akula. Petrol sometimes available at Catholic Mission at Lisala. (Ferry available on certain days, up river to Kisangani.) 323 km (201 mls)	
LISALA	Road deteriorates after leaving Lisala, with very deep twisting ruts, gullies and potholes. Average speed 32–40 kph (20–25 mph). Improves after Alberta but still very corrugated, continuing on two narrow ruts in places, overhung on each side with long grass. 169 km (105 mls)	
BUMBA	Continues as two narrow ruts overhung with thick bush, badly corrugated in places. 454 km (282 mls)	
BUTA	Total: 1195 km (742½ mls)	

BUTA	Branch Route ⇨	MAMBASA

⬇

Dirt surfaced road, rutted and potholed in places, winding through dense jungle crossing the river Arumwimi at Banalia by ferry. No petrol on route.

192 km (120 mls)

BANALIA

Road continues through dense jungle and by some plantations nearer to Kisangani. Corrugations and potholes in road, bad in places, remainder of rivers bridged. There are no facilities on this route and extra petrol should be carried.

129 km (80 mls)

KISANGANI

Good dirt road with rough section near Madula and a short section of tar around Batama. No petrol on route.

339 km (210½ mls)

NIA NIA

Improved dirt road, potholed and corrugated in places. Average speed about 40 kph (25 mph). No petrol on route.

195 km (121 mls)

MAMBASA

Total: 855 km (531½ mls)

190

BUMBA	Branch Route ⟳	MAMBASA

⬇

Fairly good road but in places just two narrow ruts overhung on each side by long grass. Free ferry at Lolo.

267 km (166 mls)

BASOKO

Take ferry across River Zaire, very good, efficient, free and takes three-quarters of an hour. Road to Elisabetha is uphill and in wet weather could be impassable. Last 32 km (20 mls) to Isangi very slow with many ruts and potholes. Road passes through swamps over numerous bridges, which should be reconnoitred on foot to ensure vehicle will pass over without being guided.

135 km (84 mls)

ISANGI

Ferry quicker and free. A fairly fast road wide enough for two vehicles, surface potholed and corrugated in places. Petrol available at Kisangani.

130 km (81 mls)

KISAN-GANI

Total: 532 km (331 mls)

Special Note: Kinshasa—Kisingani via Bangui (riverboat)

Because of the lack of suitable roads between Kinshasa and the interior road network to or from east and south Africa, a journey to or from Kinshasa is only possible by riverboat. Motorists may join this riverboat at Bangui or at Kisangani. Timetables, regulations, and approximate costs for vehicle and passengers are given in Appendix II, p. 233–234.

E4b

SERON-ERA		
Branch Route ⇨		**NAIROBI**

⇩

A hard dirt road north from Seronera towards the Kenya border. Report to customs/immigration at Lobo Lodge and cross frontier and enter the Masi Mara Reserve. A toll is payable of about 30 shillings per vehicle including two passengers plus 15 shillings for each additional passenger. A good dirt road to Narok, report to Kenya customs/immigration there.

234 km (145 mls)

TANZANIA
+ + + + + +
KENYA

NAROK

A fairly good dirt road which joins the main tarmac highway to Nairobi and proceeds through a valley and up over a scenic escarpment. Road works may be met for the road is to be tarred throughout. All facilities in Nairobi.

148 km (92 mls)

NAIROBI

Total: 382 km (237 mls)

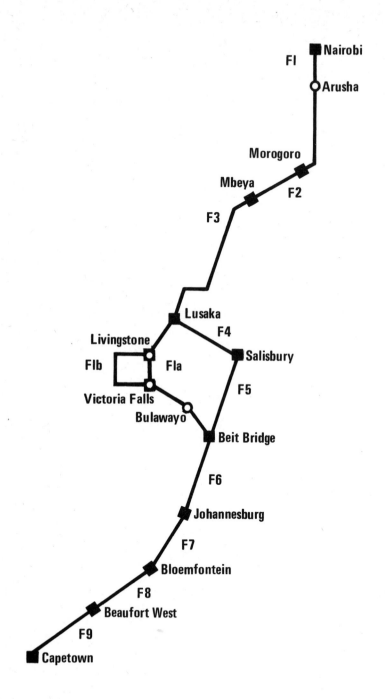

Nairobi

F1

Arusha

Morogoro

Mbeya

F2

F3

Lusaka

F4

Livingstone

F1b

F1a

Salisbury

Victoria Falls

F5

Bulawayo

Beit Bridge

F6

Johannesburg

F7

Bloemfontein

F8

Beaufort West

F9

Capetown

Part 11
East and South Africa:
North—South Routes and
Information

Trunk Routes		km	mls
F1	Nairobi—Morogoro	899	658
F2	Morogoro—Mbeya	692	430
F3	Mbeya—Lusaka	1003	623
F4	Lusaka—Salisbury	489	303
F5	Salisbury—Beit Bridge	593	369
F6	Beit Bridge—Johannesburg	560	348
F7	Johannesburg—Bloemfontein	420	261
F8	Bloemfontein—Beaufort West	555	345
F9	Beaufort West—Cape Town	489	304
	Total:	5700	3641

Alternative Route
F1a Lusaka—Beit Bridge via
Livingstone/Bulawayo 1248 775

Branch Route
F1b Livingstone—Victoria Falls
via Botswana 132 82

| **NAIROBI** | **Trunk Route** ⬦ | **CAPE TOWN** |

⬇

| **KENYA** +++++ **TANZANIA** | An all-weather road with tarmac surface throughout. Petrol available at Athi River 29 km (18 mls), Kajiado 79 km (49 mls), Bissel 111 km (69 mls), Namanga 169 km (105 mls), Longido 273 km (170 mls), and Sambu 245 km (152 mls). Kenya frontier control check-point at Namanga. Tanzania frontier control/police/immigration at Longido. All facilities at Arusha. Driving time from Nairobi 5 hours.

277 km (172 mls) |

| **ARUSHA** | An all-weather road via Himo with tarmac surface throughout. Beware of lorries being driven at high speed. Petrol available at Moshi 79 km (49 mls), Himo 108 km (67 mls), Same 188 km (117 mls) and Mombo 314 km (195 mls). All facilities at Korogwe. Driving time 5 hours.

359 km (223 mls) |

| **KOROGWE** | An all-weather road via Chalinze with tarmac surface throughout. Caution: game in surrounding countryside may stray across road. Petrol available at Msata 159 km (99 mls) and Chalinze 196 km (122 mls). Care should be taken of cattle, native buses and lorries being driven at speed on the wrong side of the road. All facilities at Morogoro. Driving time 3¼ hours.

263 km (163 mls) |

| **MORO-GORO** | **Total: 899 km (658 mls)** |

MORO-GORO	Trunk Route ⇨	CAPE TOWN

⇩

An all-weather road with tarmac surface passing through the Mikum National Park, with some rough broken tarmac surfaces. In the flat area near the Ruaha River there are many 'blind' corners. Petrol available at Mikum, 119 km (74 mls). All facilities at Iringa. Driving time 4½ hours. But time should be allowed for holdups on sections of road under reconstruction after the Ruaha River, where road may be closed by barriers from 10.00 am. to 4.00 pm. daily except Sundays and public holidays.

298 km (185 mls)

IRINGA

All-weather road with tarmac surface. Some sections are under reconstruction and may be only rough hard dirt causing clouds of dust. There are numerous bridges and drifts. The road approaching Mbeya runs through the Porotos Mountains and through interesting and beautiful countryside. Look out for sandpatches en route. Petrol available at Iheme 35 km (22 mls), Sao Hill 84 km (52 mls), Makambako 190 km (118 mls) and Chimala 298 km (185 mls). All facilities at Mbeya. Driving time 6½ hours.

394 km (245 mls)

MBEYA

Total: 692 km (430 mls)

MBEYA	Trunk Route ⇨	CAPE TOWN

TANZANIA
++++++
ZAMBIA

All-weather road with tarmac surface. Some sections are under reconstruction and may be only rough hard dirt. Tanzanian frontier/customs/police at Tunduma, 82 km (51 mls). All facilities. Zambian customs/police across frontier. Nakonde, 111 km (69 mls): no facilities. Petrol available at Isoka 191 km (119 mls): fill up as there will be no more until Mpika, which has hotel and petrol. Driving time 7 hours.

487 km (303 mls)

MPIKA

All-weather road with tarmac surface. Petrol available at Mkushi, 335 km (208 mls). Reserve should be carried on this section. All facilities at Lusaka. Driving time 7 hours.

516 km (320 mls)

LUSAKA — **Total: 1003 km (623 mls)**

F4

LUSAKA | **Trunk Route** ▷ | **CAPE TOWN**

⇩

ZAMBIA
+ + + + + +
RHODESIA

All-weather road with tarmac surface passing through attractive hilly country and undulating bush. Zambian frontier/customs at the Otto Bridge, crossing the River Zambezi 135 km (84 mls). Rhodesian customs/immigration at Chirundu, south side of river. Petrol available at Chirundu 137 km (85 mls), and Sinoia 375 km (233 mls). All facilities at Salisbury. Driving time 7 hours.

SALIS- BURY

Total: 489 km (303 mls)

Tar ■ ■ Gravel ⠿ Earth =⁼ Desert		**F5**
SALIS-BURY	**Trunk Route** ⇨	**CAPE TOWN**

⇩

A good tarred road throughout passing through undulating highland countryside descending over the last 58 km (36 mls) to Fort Victoria. All facilities en route at Enkeldoorn 151 km (94 mls), Umvuma 201 km (125 mls) and Fort Victoria.

306 km (190 mls)

FORT VICTORIA

A good tarred road throughout passing at first through hilly, partly wooded countryside to Lundi. Hotel and petrol 600 yds west of road.

109 km (68 mls)

LUNDI

Continuing good tar road via Nuanetsi passing through flat savanna and bush. All facilities Beit Bridge. Report to Rhodesian customs/immigration post which stands at northern end of bridge over Limpopo River.

178 km (111 mls)

BEIT BRIDGE

Total: 593 km (369 mls)

BEIT BRIDGE	Trunk Route ⇨	CAPE TOWN

⇩

RHODESIA + + + + + + SOUTH AFRICAN REPUBLIC	Report to South African customs/immigration 1 mile after crossing bridge. Continue on excellent tarred road passing over picturesque undulating mountainous countryside covered by forests and bush. Many magnificent views. Petrol available at Messina, Louis Trichard 111 km (69 mls) and Bandelierkop. All facilities at Pietersburg. 224 km (139 mls)
PIETERS-BURG	Excellent tarred road passing through picturesque undulating and hilly countryside. Petrol available throughout. All facilities at Warmbaths. 180 km (112 mls)
WARM-BATHS	Excellent tarred road throughout passing through flat to undulating countryside to Pretoria 100 km (62 mls) gradually climbing on the last 56 km (35 mls) to Johannesburg on dual carriageway. All facilities. 156 km (97 mls)
JOHANNES-BURG	**Total: 560 km (348 mls)**

F7

JOHANNES-BURG	Trunk Route ▷	CAPE TOWN

⬇

PARYS

Excellent tarred road gradually descending through picturesque countryside. Proceed via Baddrif bridge over Vaal river on leaving Verceniging. All facilities en route.

119 km (74 mls)

Excellent tarred road traversing picturesque, undulating to flat open high savanna. All facilities en route.

90 km (56 mls)

KROONSTAD

Excellent tarred road via Vendersburg and Winburg passing through flat to undulating countryside. Last 17 km (10 mls) on dual carriageway. All facilities en route.

211 km (131 mls)

BLOEM-FONTEIN

Total: 420 km (261 mls)

BLOEM-FONTEIN	Trunk Route ⇨	CAPE TOWN
⬇		
	Excellent tarred road traversing featureless high savanna country. All facilities en route. 122 km (76 mls)	
TROMPS-BURG	Excellent tarred road gradually climbing to Philippolie and descending to Colesburg. All facilities en route. 113 km (70 mls)	
COLESBURG	Excellent flat tarred road passing over a high plateau via Hanover and Richmond. All facilities en route. 269 km (167 mls)	
NELSPOORT	Excellent tarred road continuing over the high plateau with magnificent views of the Nuweveld range to the north of Beaufort West. 51 km (32 mls)	
BEAUFORT WEST	Total: 555 km (345 mls)	

BEAUFORT WEST	Trunk Route ⇨	CAPE TOWN

⇩

Excellent tarred road gradually descending to Prince Albert Road. All facilities en route.

119 km (74 mls)

PRINCE ALBERT ROAD

Excellent tarred road passing at first through open high plateau country, gradually climbing towards the Hex River Mountains and descending sharply to Worcester. Magnificent scenery; all facilities en route.

243 km (151 mls)

WORCESTER

Excellent tarred road winding through mountainous countryside and the magnificent Du Toits Kloof Pass, after which it descends rapidly into the undulating pastoral countryside between Paarl and Cape Town. All facilities en route.

127 km (79 mls)

CAPE TOWN

Total: 489 km (304 mls)

LUSAKA	**Alternative Route** ⇨	**CAPE TOWN**

⇩

All-weather road with tarmac surface throughout. Petrol available at Kafue, Mazabuka, Pemba, Kalomo and Zimba. All facilities at Livingstone. Driving time 7 hours.

473 km (293 mls)

LIVING-STONE
ZAMBIA
+ + + + + +
RHODESIA

Report to Zambian customs/immigration and cross bridge over Zambezi River. Report to Rhodesian customs/immigration on south side and proceed to Victoria Falls.

11 km (7 mls)

VICTORIA FALLS

Good tarred road passing through hilly countryside to Wankie and through dense bush towards Lupane. All facilities en route.

270 km (168 mls)

LUPANE

Good tarred road passing through undulating bush countryside. Petrol available at Kenmaur. Bulawayo has all facilities.

172 km (107 mls)

BULAWAYO

Good tarred road passing through bush countryside. Facilities en route at Exsexvale, Balla Balla, Gwanda, West Nicholson and Tods Hotel 120 km (75 mls) north of Beit Bridge.

322 km (200 mls)

BEIT BRIDGE

Total: 1248 km (775 mls)

F1b

LIVING-STONE	Branch Route ▷	VICTORIA FALLS

⬇

Note: This alternative route may be used whenever the Zambian/Rhodesian border posts are closed to traffic.

ZAMBIA + + + + + + BOTSWANA	Clear Zambian customs/immigration before leaving Livingstone. Leave on Mambova road and proceed on 2-lane dirt road for about 64 km (40 mls) to the Kazungula Ferry. (Ignore sign to Kazungula village.) Cross river Zambezi to Kasane on free ferry. 66 km (41 mls)

KAZUNGULA **KASANE** BOTSWANA + + + + + + RHODESIA	Report to and clear Botswana customs/immigration and proceed on dirt road to Rhodesian frontier and cross. Report to Rhodesian customs/immigration. Frontier closed 18.00 hours daily. Continue on dirt road. Some sections corrugated. All facilities at Victoria Falls. 66 km (41 mls)

VICTORIA FALLS	**Total: 132 km (82 mls)**

Part 12
Important Addresses

representatives of African governments in London, p. 211 British, Irish, Australian, Canadian and American Embassies, High Commissions and Consulates in Africa, p. 214 motoring organisations in Africa, p. 225

Representatives of African Governments in London

ALGERIA:
Embassy,
6 Hyde Park Gate, SW7.
Tel: 01-584 9502

ANGOLA:
Portuguese Consulate
General,
62 Brompton Road, SW3.
Tel: 01-235 6216

BOTSWANA:
High Commission,
3 Buckingham Gate, SW1.
Tel: 01-828 0445/6/7

BURUNDI:
None.
Nearest Embassy:
11a Rue Van Eyck,
Brussels 1, Belgium.
Tel: 47 86 02

CAMEROUN:
Embassy,
84 Holland Park, W11.
Tel: 01-727 0771

CENTRAL AFRICAN
REPUBLIC:
French Consulate General,
24 Rutland Gate, SW7.
Tel: 01-584 9628

CONGO (Brazzaville):
None.
Nearest Embassy:

57 bis Rue Scheffer,
Paris 16, France.
Tel: 727 77 09

DAHOMEY:
None.
Nearest Embassy:
89 Rue de Cherche-Midi,
Paris 6, France.
Tel: 548 58 43

EGYPT:
Embassy,
19 Palace Gardens, W8.
Tel: 01-229 8810/8/9

ETHIOPIA:
Embassy,
17 Prince's Gate, SW7.
Tel: 01-589 7212

FRENCH TERRITORY OF
THE AFAR AND ISSA:
French Consulate General,
24 Rutland Gate, SW7.
Tel: 01-584 9628

GABON:
Embassy,
66 Drayton Gardens, SW10.
Tel: 01-370 6441/2

THE GAMBIA:
High Commission,
The Gambia House,
28 Kensington Court, W8.
Tel: 01-937 0800

GHANA:
High Commission,
13 Belgrave Square, SW1.
Tel: 01-235 4142

GUINEA:
None.
Nearest Embassy:
Via Luigi Luciani 41,
00197 Rome, Italy.
Tel: 872007 804 505

IVORY COAST:
Embassy,
2 Upper Belgrave St., SW1.
Tel: 01-235 6991

KENYA:
High Commission,
Kenya House,
45 Portland Place, W1.
Tel: 01-636 2371

LESOTHO:
High Commission,
16a St. James's St., SW1.
Tel: 01-839 1154

LIBERIA:
Embassy,
21 Prince's Gate, SW7.
Tel: 01-589 9405

LIBYA:
Embassy,
58 Prince's Gate, SW7.
Tel: 01-589 5235/7

MALAWI:
High Commission,
47 Gt. Cumberland Place, W1.
Tel: 01-723 6021

MALI:
None.
Nearest Embassy:
89 Rue du Cherche-Midi,
Paris 6, France.
Tel: 548 58 43

MAURITANIA:
None.
Nearest Embassy:
5 Rue de Montevideo,
Paris 16, France.
Tel: 504 88 54

MOROCCO:
Embassy:
49 Queen's Gate Gdns., SW7.
Tel: 01-584 8827

MOZAMBIQUE:
None. Refer to:
Portuguese Consulate
General,
62 Brompton Rd., SW3.
Tel: 01-235 6216

NIGER:
None.
Nearest Embassy:
154 Rue de Longchamps,
Paris 16, France.
Tel: Trocadero 8060

NIGERIA:
High Commission,
(Visas and Passports),
178 Gt. Portland St., W1.
Tel: 01-580 8611
Information Section,
Nigeria House,
9 Northumberland Ave., WC2.
Tel: 01-839 1244

RWANDA:
None.
Nearest Embassy:
101 Boul. Saint Michel,
Brussels 4, Belgium.
Tel: 02 34 17 63

SENEGAL:
Embassy,
11 Phillimore Gardens, W8.
Tel: 01-937 3139

SIERRA LEONE:
High Commission,
33 Portland Place, W1.
Tel: 01-636 6483

SOMALI:
Embassy,
60 Portland Place, W1.
Tel: 01-580 7148/9

SOUTH AFRICA:
Embassy,
South Africa House,
Trafalgar Square, WC2.
Tel: 01-930 4488

SUDAN:
Embassy,
3 Cleveland Row,
St. James's, SW1.
Tel: 01-839 8080

SWAZILAND:
High Commission,
58 Pont St., SW1.
Tel: 01-589 5447/8

TANZANIA:
High Commission,
33 Upper Brook St., W1.

Tel: 01-499 8951

TCHAD:
French Consulate General,
24 Rutland Gate, SW7.
Tel: 01-584 9628

TOGO:
None.
Nearest Embassy:
Ave. du Tervuren 264,
Brussels 1150, Belgium.

TUNISIA:
Embassy,
20 Prince's Gate, SW7.
Tel: 01-584 8117

UGANDA:
High Commission,
Uganda House,
58–9 Trafalgar Square, WC2.
Tel: 01-839 1963

UPPER VOLTA:
None.
Nearest Embassy:
159 Boul. Haussman,
Paris, France.
Tel: 359 9063 64; 359 2185 86

ZAIRE:
Embassy,
26 Chesham Place, SW1.
Tel: 01-235 6137

ZAMBIA:
High Commission,
7–11 Cavendish Place, W1.
Tel: 01-580 0691

British, Irish, Australian, Canadian and American Embassies, High Commissions and Consulates in Africa

	ALGERIA	BOTSWANA
BRITISH (New Zealand passport holders should also apply to British representatives)	Residence Cassiopee, Batiment B, 7 Chemin des Clycines, Algiers. Tel: 9502/5	
IRISH		
AUSTRALIAN		c/o Pretoria South Africa
CANADIAN	27 Bis rue d'Anjou, Hydra, Algiers. Tel: 60 61 90/91/92	c/o Pretoria, South Africa
AMERICAN	Villa Mektoub, 4 Chemin Cheikh Bachir Brahimi, Algiers. Tel: 60 14 25/29; 60 37 70/72 (also Oran)	Koh-i-Nor House, The Mall, P.O. Box 90, Gaborone. Tel: 2944/5

CAMEROUN	CENTRAL AFRICAN REPUBLIC	DAHOMEY
Le Concorde, Ave. J. F. Kennedy, B.P. 547, Yaounde. Tel: 220545	S.C.K.N., P.O. Box 809, Bangui. Tel: 21 66/7	c/o Lome, Togo
Immeuble Soppo Priso, rue Conrad-Adenauer, P.O. Box 572, Yaounde. Tel: 22 02 03; 22 29 22; 22 19 36;	c/o Yaounde, Cameroun	c/o Accra, Ghana
B.P. 817, Rue Nachtigal, Yaounde. Tel: 33 57; 33 58	Place de la Republique Centrafricaine, Bangui. Tel: 2050; 2051	Rue Caporal Anani Bernard, Cotonou. Tel: 26 93

	EGYPT	GHANA
BRITISH (N.Z. also)	Kasr El Doubara, Garden City, Cairo. Tel: 20850/9	Barclays Bank Building, High Street, P.O. Box 296, Accra. Tel: 64651
IRISH		Honorary Consul, Donal P. Crilly, Ghana Aluminium Products Ltd., P.O. Box 124, Tema.
AUSTRALIAN	1097 Corniche el Nil, Garden City, Cairo. Tel: 28190, 28663, 22862	Milne Close, Off Dr. Amilcar Cabral Road, Airport Residential Area, P.O. Box 2445, Accra. Tel: 77972, 75671/2
CANDIAN	6 Sharia Mohammed Fahmed el Sayed, Garden City, Cairo. (Post: Kasr el Doubara P.O.) Tel: 2 31 10	E 115/3 Independence Avenue, P.O. Box 1639, Accra. Tel: 28555, 28502
AMERICAN	5 Sharia Latin America, Cairo. Tel: 28219 (also Alexandria)	P.O. Box 194, Liberia & Rowe Roads, Accra. Tel: 66811

IVORY COAST	KENYA	LIBYA
Immeuble Shell, Avenue Lamblin, P.O. Box 2581, Abidjan. Tel: 22 66 15; 32 29 80; 32 27 76	Bruce House, Standard Street, P.O. Box 48543, Nairobi. Tel: 35944	30 Tariq Al Fatah, Tripoli. Tel: 31191
	Honorary Consul, Edward D. O'Loghlen, P.O. Box 30310, Nairobi.	
	AFC/ADC Building, Development House, Government Road, P.O. Box 30360, Nairobi. Tel: 35666; 34672 Telex: 22203 Austcom	
Immeuble 'Le General', 4eme et 5eme etages, avenue Botreau-Roussel B.P. 21194 Abidjan. Tel: 32 20 09	Industrial Promotion Services Building, Kimathi Street, P.O. Box 30481, Nairobi. Tel: 34033/4/5/6	c/o Cairo, Egypt
5 Rue Jesse Owens, P.O. Box 1712, Abidjan. Tel: 32 46 30	P.O. Box 30137, Cotts House, Eliot Street, Nairobi. Tel: 35141	Garden City, Shari'al-Nsr, Tripoli. Tel: 34021; 32026

	MALI	MALAWI
BRITISH (N.Z. also)	Rue Guegnan, B.P. 110, Bamako. Tel: 23 56; 33 56	
IRISH		Honorary Consul, Richard F. Fitzsimons, P.O. Box 462, Downs House, Victoria Avenue, Blantyre.
AUSTRALIAN		
CANADIAN	c/o Dakar, Senegal	c/o Lusaka, Zambia
AMERICAN	Rue Testard & Rue Mohamed V, Bamako. Tel: 4663; 4834	

MAURITANIA	MOROCCO	NIGER
'Somima', B.P. 275, Nouakchott. Tel: 23 27	28 bis Avenue Allal Ben Abdullah, B.P. 45, Rabat. Tel: 20905/6; 31403/4; 32296;	c/o Abidjan, Ivory Coast
c/o Dakar, Senegal	13 Bis, Rue des Cadets de Samur, Rabat-Agdal. (B.P. 553, Rabat-Chellah) Tel: 713 75/6	c/o Abidjan, Ivory Coast
B.P. 222, Nouakchott. Tel: 20 60	2 Avenue de Marrakech, Rabat. Tel: 3036/2 (also Tangiers)	B.P. 201, Niamey. Tel: 2670; 2664

	NIGERIA	RWANDA
BRITISH (N.Z. also)	Western House, 8 Gowon Street, Lagos. Tel: 51630	
IRISH	New Africa House, 4th Floor, 31 Marina, P.O. Box 2421, Lagos.	
AUSTRALIAN	Investment House (4th Floor), 21/25 Yakubu Gowon Street, P.O. Box 2427, Lagos. Tel: 25981/2	
CANADIAN	Niger House, Tinubu Street, P.O. Box 851, Lagos. Tel: 53630/1/2/3/4	c/o Kinshasa, Zaire
AMERICAN	1 King's College Rd., Lagos. Tel: 57320/8 (also Ibadan, Kaduna)	13 Blvd Central, Kigali. Tel: 5601

SENEGAL	REPUBLIC OF SOUTH AFRICA	SUDAN
20 Rue du Docteur Guillet, B.P. 6025, Dakar. Tel: 22383	B.P. Centre, Kerk/Harrison Streets, P.O. Box 10101, Johannesburg. Tel: 834 6411 (also Cape Tn, Durban, Pt. Eliz., P'toria, Windhiek)	New Aboulela Building, Barlaman Avenue, P.O. Box 801, Khartoum. Tel: 70760; 70766/9
	Honorary Consul, Patrick Ryan, 9/10 London House, 21 Loveday Street, Johannesburg.	
	3°2 Standard Bank Chambers, Church Square, Pretoria. Tel: 3 7051, 3 4778 (also Cape Tn., Jo'burg)	c/o Cairo, Egypt
45 avenue de la Republique, P.O. Box 3373, Dakar. Tel: 20270	P.O. Box 26006, Arcadia, Pretoria. Tel: 487062/3/4 (also Cape Tn., Jo'burg)	c/o Cairo, Egypt
B.P. 49, BIAO Bldg., Place de l'Independance, Dakar. Tel: 26344/5; 22143	Thibault House, 225 Pretorius Street, Pretoria. Tel: 48 4266 (also Jo'burg)	P.O. Box 699, Gambouria Avenue, Khartoum. Tel: 74700; 74611

	TANZANIA	TCHAD
BRITISH (N.Z. also)	Permanent House, Azikwe Street/ Independence Ave., P.O. Box 9200, Dar-es-Salaam. Tel: 29601/7;	Conoco, B.P. 694, Ndjamena (Fort Lamy) Tel: 3202
IRISH	Honorary Consul, James B. Wallrab, P.O. Box 9102, Dar-es-Salaam.	
AUSTRALIAN	Bank House (4th Floor), Independence Avenue, P.O. Box 2996, Dar-es-Salaam. Tel: 20244/5/6	
CANADIAN	Pan Africa Insurance Building, Independence Ave., P.O. Box 1022, Dar-es-Salaam. Tel: 20651	c/o Yaounde, Cameroun
AMERICAN	National Bank of Commerce Bldg., on City Drive, P.O. Box 9123 Dar-es-Salaam. Tel: 22775 (also Zanzibar)	Rue du Lt Col Colonna d'Ornano, B.P. 413, Ndjamena. Tel: 3091/2/3/4

TOGO	TUNISIA	UGANDA
Boulevard Circulaire, Lome. Tel: 2085 Telex: 5210 a/b Prodrome Lome	5 Place de la Victoire, Tunis. Tel: 245 100; 245 324; 245 649	Parliament Avenue, P.O. Box 7070, Kampala. Tel: 57054/9
		c/o Nairobi Kenya
c/o Accra, Ghana	2 Place Virgile, Notre-Dame de Tunis, P.O. Box 606, Tunis. Tel: 284950; 286619; 286114	c/o Nairobi, Kenya
Rue Pelletier Caventor & rue Vauban, Lome. Tel: 2991	144 Ave. de la Liberte, Tunis. Tel: 282 566; 282 549; 258 559	

	ZAIRE	ZAMBIA
BRITISH (N.Z. also)	Avenue de l'Equateur, B.P. 8049, Kinshasa. Tel: 23483	Independence Avenue, P.O. Box RW 50, Lusaka. Tel: 51122
IRISH		Honorary Consul, Conor J. MacIntyre, P.O. Box 338, Lusaka.
AUSTRALIAN		c/o Dar-es-Salaam, Tanzania
CANADIAN	Edifice Shell, coin av. Wangata et boul. du 30-juin, P.O. Box 8341, Kinshasa. Tel: 22706; 24346	Barclays Bank North End Branch, Cairo Road, Lusaka. Tel: 75187/8
AMERICAN	310 Ave. des Aviateurs, Kinshasa. Tel: 25881/6 (also Lubumbashi, Bukavu)	David Livingstone Rd & Independence Ave., P.O. Box 1617, Lusaka. Tel: 50222

Motoring Organisations in Africa

ALGERIA:
Automobile Club National
D'Algerie,
99 Boulevard Bouskouir,
B.P. 67 – Alger Gare.
Tel: 64 97 71

EGYPT:
Automobile et Touring Club
D'Egypte,
10 Rue Kasr-El-Nil,
Le Caire.
Tel: 77241/2/3; 77340

GHANA:
Automobile Association,
Fanum Place,
National Liberation Square,
P.O. Box 1985, Accra.

KENYA:
Automobile Association of
East Africa,
A.A. House, Westlands,
P.O. Box 40087, Nairobi.
Tel: 46826

LIBYA:
Automobile and Touring Club
of Libya,
Al Fath Boulevard,
Maidan al-Ghazala,
P.O. Box 3566, Tripoli.
Tel: 33310; 33515; 33066

MALAWI:
Automobile Association of
Rhodesia,
Blantyre Insurance and
General Agencies,
Victoria Avenue,
P.O. Box 333, Blantyre.
Tel: 2331

MOROCCO:
Royal Automobile Club
Morocain,
Place des Nations Unies,
B.P. 94, Casablanca.
Tel: 613 11

RHODESIA:
Automobile Association of
Rhodesia,
Fanum House,
57 Jameson Avenue Central,
P:O. Box 585, Salisbury C.I.
Tel: 61121

SENEGAL:
Automobile Club du Senegal,
Immeuble Chambre de
Commerce,
Place de l'Independance,
B.P. 295, Dakar.
Tel: 266 04 8

SOUTH AFRICA:
Automobile Association of
South Africa,
A.A. House, 42 De Villiers
Street,
P.O. Box 596, Johannesburg.

TANZANIA:
Automobile Association of
East Africa,
P.O. Box 3004,
Dar-es-Salaam.

TUNISIA:
National Automobile Club de
Tunisie,
29 Avenue Habib Bourguiba,
Tunis.
Tel: 243 921; 241 176

ZAIRE:
Fédération Automobile du
Zaire,
Building Forescom,
118 Avenue du Port,
B.P. 263, Kinshasa.

ZAMBIA:
Automobile Association of
Zambia,
Stand 1020, Cairo Road,
Lusaka.
(also at Kitwe and
Livingstone)

Appendices

Appendix I
Motoring through the Sudan

If you intend to motor through the Sudan, you should make sure that the following forms are correctly filled in and approved by the Sudanese authorities *before* you begin your journey. If you intend to travel in convoy, the form headed 'Motoring in unaccompanied vehicle' obviously does not apply. Details on where to send the forms and how much time to allow are given on page 35.

Application Form

This must be filled in by *all* motorists wishing to travel through the Sudan.

1. The make and horse-power of the car or motor-cycle:
2. Particulars of any special equipment to render it fit for desert travel:
3. Names, ages, sexes and nationality of all members of the party, and which of them are qualified drivers and/or driver mechanics:
4. The reason the journey is being undertaken:
5. Date and place of entry into the Sudan, together with an itinerary of your journey and final destination:
6. Whether you are prepared to deposit the sum of £S.100 in respect of every member of the party with a Bank. We also require a guarantee from the Bank that they are holding this money on behalf of the Sudan Government until such a time as you have passed through Sudan territory:
7. Whether the car is insured in respect of Third Party Risks, and in case this is not so we enclose a list of recognised insurers in the Sudan:
8. Whether you are prepared to sign an undertaking in the form of the attached, which should be returned to this Office:

Signature ....
Address ....
Date: ....

General Undertaking

This Undertaking must be signed by all persons intending to enter and travel in or through the Sudan by motor-vehicles.

1. I .... of ....
in consideration of the grant to me by the Sudan Government of a visa or permit to enter the Sudan hereby undertake with the Sudan Government as follows:

Before reaching, and after leaving, Sudan territory, to comply with all such regulations and instructions as may from time to time be applied by the Governments of territories adjacent to the Sudan to persons travelling by motor vehicle in such territories.

If travelling to the Sudan from the North through Egypt:

(a) To produce my motor vehicle for examination by the Sudan Ambassador or his authorised representative, and certification by him that the said motor vehicle is in all respects reasonably fit, and is sufficiently equipped with essential spares, for the proposed journey.

(b) Not to travel between Shellal and Wadi Halfa except in a convoy consisting of not less than two motor vehicles.

On reaching the Sudan frontier whether from Egypt or any other adjacent territory, to produce my motor-vehicle for similar examination and certification by the District Commissioner or his authorised representative.

Not to proceed in such motor-vehicle from Cairo to the Sudan, or from any Sudan frontier into the Sudan, as the case may be, unless and until such certificate has been granted.

While proceeding through the Sudan, to report my arrival and departure to the District Commissioner in each district through which I travel by motor vehicle.

To comply with all such instructions as may be given me by the District Commissioner, while travelling by motor vehicle through his district, including instructions as to what food and water supplies and equipment and spares are to be carried, what route is to be followed, and what arrangements for convoy if any are to be made.

If travelling to Egypt from the Sudan through the Sudan, not to travel between Wadi Halfa and Shellal except in a convoy consisting of not less than two motor vehicles.

2. I hereby authorise the Sudan Government to conduct on my behalf such search, rescue, salvage or transport operations, and to incur in respect thereof such expenses as it may think fit, and I undertake to repay to the Sudan Government on demand the whole or a reasonable proportion (such reasonable proportion to be certified by the Governor of the Province concerned, whose decision shall be final) of the costs of such operations.

By way of security or partial security for the payment of any sums that may become due from me to the Sudan Government under the preceding sub-clause, or otherwise under this agreement, I undertake to enter the payment of such sum and with sureties as the Sudan Government may require, viz £S.100 per person.

3. I hereby acknowledge and agree:

That I shall not have any claim against the Sudan Government or the official concerned for any costs, damages or expenses which may be occasioned to me by the refusal whether temporary or permanent of a certificate under Clause 1, 2 or 3 hereof.

That in the event of my proceeding or endeavouring to proceed by motor-vehicle without obtaining the said certificate, the Sudan Government shall be entitled to revoke the said visa or permit, and I shall not have any claim against the Sudan Government for any costs, damages or expenses which may be occasioned to me by such revocation.

That the Sudan Government shall be under no obligation to conduct on my behalf any of the operations specified in the preceding clause, whether or not I shall have committed any breach of the undertakings on my part herein contained.

That this agreement shall be construed according to the laws of the Sudan for the time being in force and shall be enforceable in the Sudan Courts.

Witness.   Signature of traveller.

Motoring in an unaccompanied Vehicle

I ....
of ....
have been informed by the Sudan Embassy in London, that the

Sudan Government strongly advise a minimum of two four-wheeled Motor Vehicles for travelling through the Sudan, owing to the risk of breakdown in uninhabited country. I still propose, however, to proceed with one vehicle.

Signature ....
Address ....
Date : ....

Specimen Letter of Guarantee for Motorists

By this bond we .... (name of obligor)
of ....(address) hereinafter
called the obligor and ....
(name of surety) of...
(address) hereinafter called the surety are held and firmly bound
jointly and severally to .... on
behalf of the Sudan Government. Signed and sealed in our respective
names this..day of..

Whereas the Sudan Government have agreed to grant the obligor a visa or permit to enter the Sudan upon the obligor and the surety entering into a bond in the sum of..for the due performance and observance of the stipulations, provisions and conditions to be performed and observed and contained in an agreement dated..and made between the obligor and the Sudan Government.

Now the condition of the above written bond is such that it is to be void in case the above bonder shall henceforth at all times perform and observe the stipulations, provisions and conditions on his part to be performed and observed and contained in the agreement hereinafter mentioned and made between him and the Sudan Government.

Signed and sealed ....

Appendix II
Zaire River Transport: Kinshasa—Kisangani

The Zaire riverboat service is operated by Onatra, Gare Fluviale: B.P. 747 Kinshasa, Tel: 24639 and B.P. 162 Kisangani, Tel: 254. Regulations and formalities for embarkation of passengers, vehicles and baggage are as follows:

Embarkation at River Station

Couriers I.T.B. Fleuve Line No. 1 Onatra departs weekly on Mondays from Kinshasa at 17.00 hrs; embarkation from 12.00 hrs to 16.00 hrs (gates to quay are closed at 16.00 hrs). Departs Kisangani weekly on Thursdays. Duration of travel: 9 days upstream; 5 days downstream.
Note: No access to quay for persons not in possession of tickets. Quay tickets for visitors cancelled. On leaving station, passengers must cross quay and embark immediately on boat or barge. The gangways are guarded by Onatra Security Officers. Once on board, passengers cannot return to quayside. As soon as gates are closed, no person or vehicle can be admitted to quay.

Hand Luggage (free allowance)

Hand luggage, known as cabin luggage, covers everything a passenger is able to carry making *one journey only* from the railway station to the cabin of the ship. Free allowances are as follows:

'Luxe' Class: 60 kg or 5 articles not exceeding 60 kg.
1st Class: 50 kg or 4 articles not exceeding 50 kg.
2nd Class: 40 kg or 3 articles not exceeding 40 kg.
3rd Class: 20 kg or 2 articles not exceeding 20 kg.

Cabin baggage articles cover suitcases, trunks, or travel bags, and

233

exclude any other baggage. Any articles exceeding the maximum weight are taxed at 1st Class goods tariff.

Accompanied Luggage

Everything a passenger is unable to carry on board as hand luggage in the one journey is carried in the hold of the barges under cover of a luggage list. (One cycle or moped per passenger is allowed.)

Note: For the Fleuve boat (Line No. 1), the above luggage is accepted only up to 17.00 hrs on the Friday preceding departure. After this, no article can be accepted as accompanied luggage.

Accompanied cars (lorries excluded) must be delivered at the River Station, at which time the ticket must also be produced. The manager of the River Station will note on the back of the original of the ticket:

'Convoy .... Of ....'

The station manager then adds his signature, stamp and date.*

Acceptance of the vehicle takes place at Port/Import under cover of a conveyance letter on which the ticket number is shown. This takes place at 10.00 hrs at the latest on the day of departure for I.T.B. (Fleuve Line No. 1). (There is a maximum of 15 cars per I.T.B. convoy.)

Note: The conveyance letter covering transport of an accompanied car must be shown at the taxation office for numbering, taxation and payment. For cars embarking on Line No. 1 this must be carried out by the Saturday preceding departure—at the latest.

The taxation office will only accept a letter of conveyance if the ticket shown by the passenger is endorsed (see above *).

Examples of basic fares

1st Class passenger fare: 1969.00 makuta (Zaires 19.69)
Land Rover: 12222 makuta (Zaires 122.22). (Basic rate: may be more, depending on weight.)
Rate of exchange at April 1975: Zaires 1.20 = £1 Sterling.

Appendix III
Useful Conversion Tables

Kilometres into Miles

Kms	Mls	Kms	Mls	Kms	Mls	Kms	Mls
1	0·62	31	19·26	61	37·90	91	56·54
2	1·24	32	19·88	62	38·52	92	57·16
3	1·86	33	20·50	63	39·14	93	57·79
4	2·48	34	21·12	64	39·76	94	58·41
5	3·10	35	21·74	65	40·39	95	59·03
6	3·72	36	22·37	66	41·01	96	59·65
7	4·34	37	22·99	67	41·63	97	60·27
8	4·97	38	23·61	68	42·25	98	60·89
9	5·59	39	24·23	69	42·87	99	61·51
10	6·21	40	24·85	70	43·49	100	62·14
11	6·83	41	25·47	71	44·11	200	124·28
12	7·45	42	26·09	72	44·74	300	186·42
13	8·07	43	26·72	73	45·36	400	248·56
14	8·69	44	27·34	74	45·98	500	310·70
15	9·32	45	27·96	75	46·60	600	372·84
16	9·94	46	28·58	76	47·22	700	434·98
17	10·56	47	29·20	77	47·84	800	497·12
18	11·18	48	29·82	78	48·46	900	559·26
19	11·80	49	30·44	79	49·09	1000	621·40
20	12·42	50	31·07	80	49·71		
21	13·04	51	31·69	81	50·33		
22	13·67	52	32·31	82	50·95		
23	14·29	53	32·93	83	51·57		
24	14·91	54	33·55	84	52·19		
25	15·53	55	34·17	85	52·81		
26	16·15	56	34·79	86	53·44		
27	16·77	57	35·41	87	54·06		
28	17·39	58	36·04	88	54·68		
29	18·02	59	36·66	89	55·30		
30	18·64	60	37·28	90	55·92		

Miles into Kilometres

Mls	Kms	Mls	Kms	Mls	Kms	Mls	Kms
1	1·60	17	27·35	33	53·10	49	78·85
2	3·21	18	28·96	34	54·71	50	80·46
3	4·82	19	30·57	35	56·32	55	88·51
4	6·43	20	32·18	36	57·93	60	96·55
5	8·04	21	33·79	37	59·54	65	104·60
6	9·65	22	35·40	38	61·15	70	112·65
7	11·26	23	37·01	39	62·76	75	120·69
8	12·87	24	38·62	40	64·37	80	128·74
9	14·48	25	40·23	41	65·98	85	136·79
10	16·09	26	41·84	42	67·59	90	144·83
11	17·70	27	43·45	43	69·19	95	152·88
12	19·31	28	45·06	44	70·80	100	160·93
13	20·92	29	46·66	45	72·41	200	321·86
14	22·53	30	48·27	46	74·02	300	482·79
15	24·13	31	49·88	47	75·63	400	643·72
16	25·74	32	51·48	48	77·24	500	804·65

Miles per Gallon into Kilometres per Litre

Miles per Gallon	Kilometres per Litre	Miles per Gallon	Kilometres per Litre
10	3·5	20	7·1
12	4·2	22	7·8
15	5·3	25	8·8
16	5·7	30	10·6
17	6·0	35	12·4
18	6·4	40	14·2
19	6·7	50	17·7

Driving Time over Distances in Kilometres

Distance in kilometres	20 mph hrs mins		30 mph hrs mins		40 mph hrs mins		50 mph hrs mins	
				Average miles driven per hour (mph)				
20		37		25		19		15
30		56		37		28		22
40	1	14		50		37		30
50	1	33	1	02		47		37
60	1	52	1	15		56		45
70	2	10	1	25	1	05		52
80	2	29	1	39	1	15	1	00
90	2	48	1	52	1	24	1	07
100	3	06	2	04	1	33	1	15

Metres into Feet and Feet into Metres

Metres	Feet	Metres	Feet	Feet	Metres	Feet	Metres
1	3·2	17	55·7	1	0·3	17	5·1
2	6·5	18	58·0	2	0·6	18	5·4
3	9·8	19	62·3	3	0·9	19	5·7
4	13·1	20	65·6	4	1·2	20	6·0
5	16·4	21	68·9	5	1·5	21	6·4
6	19·6	22	72·1	6	1·8	22	6·7
7	22·9	23	75·4	7	2·1	23	7·0
8	26·2	24	78·7	8	2·4	24	7·3
9	29·5	25	82·0	9	2·7	25	7·6
10	32·8	50	164·0	10	3·0	50	15·2
11	36·0	75	246·0	11	3·3	75	22·3
12	39·3	100	328·1	12	3·6	100	30·4
13	42·6	200	656·2	13	3·9	200	60·9
14	45·9	300	984·3	14	4·2	300	91·4
15	49·2	400	1312·4	15	4·5	400	121·9
16	52·4	500	1640·5	16	4·8	500	152·4

Gradients

The ascent in feet for every mile climbed on a given gradient is shown below. On many maps this is expressed as a gradient percentage, which is also shown.

Grade (feet)	Feet per mile	Percentage	Grade (feet)	Feet per mile	Percentage
1 in 5	1,056	20	1 in 15	352	6·6
1 in 6	880	16·4	1 in 16	330	6·4
1 in 7	754	14·2	1 in 17	310	5·8
1 in 8	635	12·4	1 in 18	293	5·5
1 in 9	586	11·1	1 in 19	227	5·2
1 in 10	528	10	1 in 20	264	5
1 in 11	480	9·1	1 in 25	218	4
1 in 12	440	8·4	1 in 30	155	3·3
1 in 13	406	7·9	1 in 35	151	2·8
1 in 14	337	7·2	1 in 40	132	2·5

Effect of Altitude upon Horsepower

A slight falling-off of engine performance will sometimes occur in high regions. The table below shows the reduction in horsepower that may be expected at various altitudes.

Altitude	Percentage of normal hp.
Sea Level	100
1000 ft	96·5
2000 ft	93
3000 ft	89·5
4000 ft	86
5000 ft	83
6000 ft	80
7000 ft	77·5

Tyre Pressure Equivalents

Pounds per sq in	Kilogrammes per sq cm	Atmospheres
14	0·98	0·95
16	1·12	1·08
18	1·26	1·22
20	1·40	1·36
22	1·54	1·49
24	1·68	1·63
26	1·83	1·76
28	1·96	1·90
30	2·10	2·04
32	2·24	2·16
36	2·52	2·44
40	2·80	2·72
50	3·50	3·40
55	3·85	3·74
60	4·20	4·08
65	4·55	4·42

Index